A BRIEF HISTORY OF

ANXIETY

[YOURS & MINE]

PATRICIA PEARSON

VINTAGE CANADA

VINTAGE CANADA EDITION, 2009

Copyright © 2008 Patricia Pearson

Published in Canada by Vintage Canada, a division of Random House
of Canada Limited, Toronto, in 2009. Originally published in hardcover
in Canada by Random House Canada, a division of Random House of
Canada Limited, Toronto, in 2008, and simultaneously in the United
States by Bloomsbury USA. Distributed by Random House of Canada
Limited, Toronto.

Vintage Canada and colophon are registered trademarks of Random
House of Canada Limited.

www.randomhouse.ca

Library and Archives Canada Cataloguing in Publication

Pearson, Patricia, 1964–
A brief history of anxiety (yours & mine) / Patricia Pearson.

Includes bibliographical references.
ISBN 978-0-679-31499-8

1. Pearson, Patricia, 1964–   . 2. Anxiety—History.
3. Anxiety—Patients—Canada—Biography. I. Title.
II. Title: Brief history of anxiety (yours and mine).
BF575A6P43 2009   152.4'6   C2008-903682-4

Typeset by Westchester Book Group

Printed and bound in Canada

1 3 5 7 9 10 8 6 4 2

For G.A.H.P. and K.A.P., who've been there, done that.
And for Anne, who has nourished my soul.

Contents

Let's Roll

We foresee great peril if governments and societies do not take action now to render nuclear weapons obsolete and to prevent further climate change.
—STEPHEN HAWKING, PHYSICIST AND MEMBER OF THE *BULLETIN OF THE ATOMIC SCIENTISTS* BOARD OF SPONSORS, 2007

I awoke morning after morning with a horrible dread at the pit of my stomach, and with a sense of the insecurity of life that I never knew before . . .
—WILLIAM JAMES, 1902

GIVEN MY DRUTHERS, I would prefer not to be afraid of the following: phone bills, ovarian cancer, black bears, climate change, walking on golf courses at night, being blundered into by winged insects; unseemly heights, running out of gas, having the mole on my back that I can feel, but not see, secretly morph into a malignant melanoma. Plus, flying. This is a big problem. Also, on occasion, the prospect that the supervolcano underlying Yosemite National Park will erupt and kill us all. Certainly, in addition, unexpected liver failure. And cows. Also, but only occasionally, when I'm really over the edge with anxiety, the fear that the car I'm driving will simply explode.

It is not that these fears aren't inherently valid, because *maybe they are*. One must be vigilant. One must struggle continuously with the validity of one's fears. Yet they vex me because of what I do not fear: crime, bats, house fires, social censure, terrorism, breast cancer, trans fats, and any harm coming to my two small children.

"Do I contradict myself? Very well then, I contradict myself," wrote Walt Whitman, that great American poet who was phobic of spiders. Apparently, I share this odd proclivity for contradiction with forty million adult Americans in any given year. That is an astonishing number. Nearly 20 percent of the adult inhabitants of the Land of the Brave are as anxious as I am, in one way or another, to a clinically significant degree. Phobic, some of them; others, prone to panic attacks; generalized anxiety, which is my label; somatic hysteria, posttraumatic stress disorder, obsessive compulsive disorder—an array of thorny cloaks to wear.

I like to imagine them—these forty million kindred nervous souls—experiencing the same juddering sense of alarm that I felt in January 2006 when I noticed that the U.S. Department of Health and Human Services had issued a bulletin about pandemic influenza. The warning went out via a newly dedicated Web site, pandemicflu.gov, advising the citizenry in all states to stockpile six to eight weeks' worth of food and water . . . like, *nowish*.

"But why?" I wondered, with detectable palpitations of the heart. "What's about to happen?" A Google search suggested terrible things. Vast amounts of suffering and death. Rasping, blue-in-the-face plague along the lines of the Great Influenza of 1918. A brand new pandemic that would kill pretty much everyone in the prime of their lives more or less shortly (it wasn't precisely clear when). In the winter of 2006, the virus was still busy trying to figure out how to mutate in order to infect humans more swiftly than birds, but then . . . well. That's it. You understand? Calamity.

Therefore, proclaimed pandemicflu.gov, which I had stumbled across from a random link on the Drudge Report, you really, really need to stock cans of tuna and Evian water in the basement, because at the appointed time, the clerk at the 7-Eleven will drop dead and *no one will sell you your food.*

How do I, and forty million Americans, put this? When you suffer from anxiety, which has been very aptly described as fear in search of a cause, you do not need official encouragement. Go away with your stockpile advisory, because here is what it is going to make me do:

"Patricia?" ventured my husband about a month later, having signed for a postal delivery at our door. "Are you all right?"

"Why?" I called down distractedly from my third-floor home office.

"Well," he said, coming upstairs, his even-tempered voice growing louder with each step, "last week a box with twelve containers of freeze-dried vegetables arrived at the house from a company called Survival Acres, and I meant to ask you about it, you know, but I forgot, and now you seem to have purchased a really big tin of powdered butter."

He darkened the threshold of my office, displaying the newly delivered package. "It says you need to add twenty-seven cups of water." My dear husband eyed me thoughtfully, poised somewhere between bursting out laughing and giving me a hug.

It is always thus. I catch him off guard. Ask anyone who suffers from what John Keats called "wakeful anguish," and they will assure you that their affliction isn't visible to the naked eye. The chronically anxious aren't physically timid, or cringing. We don't quake in our boots or whimper aloud as we board airplanes. In folklore and anecdote, the anxious have been conflated with the immature and emotionally uninhibited as "nervous Nellies," but the perception is a prejudice. Our fears are private, arbitrary, idiosyncratic, and very often masked. Anxiety rages undetected in the mind, both secretive and wild.

Friends and acquaintances, children, even lovers can be fooled. Who knew that Charles Darwin was struggling to suppress a rising sense of panic in his later years? Who glimpsed the dread felt by Alfred Lord Tennyson, or by W. B. Yeats? Is a face-clutching terror evident in the bold joy of Aretha Franklin as she sings, or in the elegant play of David Beckham? Yet both contend all the time with a fraught sense of balancing on the cliff's edge. I know of one CEO who gets paralyzed with terror whenever he enters a tunnel, but I doubt his business associates have noticed this when they've driven together in a limo from LaGuardia beneath the East River and into Manhattan. Another accomplished professional of my acquaintance spends her downtime silently making contingency plans for the tornado she's certain will hit her house in Montreal. One friend is a gregarious charmer, a man who soars at his job in Chicago, all the while governed by his phobia that something will snap off his toes.

You can't claim to spot an anxious person a mile away. The signals aren't that strong. Anxious people don't even recognize one another. Apprehension runs through us like an underground current; it electrifies when no one is watching.

By March 2006, the government of New Zealand had embarked upon a house-by-house mailing to all of its nationals, asking them to think seriously about an imminent outbreak of death and pestilence. I knew this because, rather than contend with the financial issues that were actually causing my anxiety, I had become a daily visitor to a Web site called Flu Wiki. Here could be found a great milling together of fiercely articulate and freaked-out people from around the world, posting to discussion topics like "What Will We Do with the Bodies?" It was like an informal or unacknowledged meeting space for Neurotics Anonymous. The conversations ranged widely, from scientific discourses on virus mutation to historic analysis of pandemics, to tips for home fuel storage—on the presumption that self-quarantine would be the only effective protection from contracting the virus.

"I've washed my hands so much this week they're bleeding," a Texan mother of seven posted to the Flu Wiki one evening. She was self-reliant and in control. She had already bought birthday and Christmas presents for her youngsters so that they would enjoy all their rituals while in quarantine. She had thought of every possibility. For anxiety is engaged in endless subsets of "what if?" and "if then." The essence of the condition is an intolerance of uncertainty. A need, as the psychologist Maria Miceli has said, "for absolute predictive control." The mother from Texas was a frequent poster to the site, and seemed to function as a maternal figure for the others. She confessed to being exhausted. I might have suggested that she had a touch of Obsessive Compulsive Disorder, what with washing her hands until they bled, but any post that implied that the community was disordered—and such posts appeared now and then—was swiftly batted away by a chorus of boos.

I read "Cooking with Canned Goods Only" with interest, feeling a certain nostalgia for pioneer days as depicted in *Little House on the Prairie*, when fears were succinct and clear and Pa had a gun. But I didn't warm to the more jangly post-apocalyptic topic "How to Prevent Home Invasions," which was based on the notion that people who had failed to prepare for the pandemic would begin searching desperately and aggressively for food. All 262 suggestions on this classic American thread were inventive in an earnest, homemade kind of way, as if Martha Stewart had developed a psychosis and put out a special issue of her magazine: crafts and cupcakes for The Followed. "Roll up towels etc. and tie them all up in plastic bags to look like the shape of a dead body and put skunk oil on it," one poster suggested. "Maybe lay the 'dead body' on pavement, or somewhere, so that the 'blood' that seems to be seeping from it is noticed."

Lest anyone on Flu Wiki begin to wonder if we were paying "selective attention to threat," as researchers say those of us with anxiety are prone to do, one could always find a supportive quotation from bird flu experts. According to the epidemiologist Michael Osterholm, director of the Center for Infectious Disease Research and Policy at the University of Minnesota, for example, if the pandemic hit that winter, "I don't know what we could do about it except say, 'We're screwed.' "

Of course. But we're screwed anyway. As I write this in the winter of 2007, scientists in London have just moved the hand on their Doomsday Clock one minute closer to midnight in order to symbolize the approach of civilization's end. I'm not sure what they want me to do in response to this dramatic ceremonial gesture, other than sigh deeply and lie down. Cover myself with crumbled autumnal leaves, perhaps, as I once witnessed an injured squirrel do in my backyard on a bone-damp November morning, remarkably effacing itself.

At least, in prepping for a flu pandemic, I can store tins of butter and plot my family's flight from an urban center. What exactly am I supposed to do about "civilization's end"? The scientists who operate the Doomsday Clock are practicing a self-defeating rhetoric that actually appeals more to the depressed than to the anxious. Anxiety distinguishes itself from depression by expressing a grim and slender hope

PATRICIA PEARSON

that one will manage to prevail. The depressed drop their briefcases, sink to their knees, and say "fuck it." The anxious pick and choose between the many vague, world-ending scenarios offered to them these days and seek out the ones they can plan around. To respond to the Doomsday Clock requires tracking down shadowy figures in international arms dealing in remote corners of central Asia and somehow preventing them from selling nuclear weapons or else the world will end; the threat of bird flu calls for a whole bunch of shopping at Target.

There are several ways to cope with dread, but I specialize in what psychologist Maria Miceli calls "hypothetical analytical planning." This is where you lie in bed at night and run through as many prospective scenarios as you can imagine and then rehearse them in French, or from the vantage point of a cat. "One's power over events is closely dependent on one's power to foresee," Miceli notes, "because if I cannot foresee, I cannot act." In order to be able to take the preventive actions required, I have to proceed in the laborious and demanding task of formulating the various hypotheses about the possible courses that events could take. And since those courses are pretty much infinite, the anxiety is never solved and simply deepens, like grooves being laid down in vinyl.

What if I can't fit

The powdered butter and dehydrated dinners

Into my Mazda? Along with the dogs and children?

Will we stay here? In the basement?

If the dogs need to go out, how will they come back in
Without bringing the virus into the home on their feet?
They might
Step in avian feces.
Shall I purchase booties?

In these times we speak a great deal about fear: the politics of fear, the culture of fear, the "gift" of fear, the fear of fear. But fear and anxiety are vitally different experiences, and it is actually anxiety that characterizes our age. Fear is invoked by immediate threat, and galvanizes a response. A bear chases you: you run away. A car hurtles out of control: you leap off the road. Terrorists hijack your flight and aim it at Washington: you say, "Let's roll."

"Fear sharpens the senses," observed the German psychiatrist Kurt Goldstein, "anxiety paralyzes them."

We perceive these two responses as if they marked a difference in character, but it's really a difference in plight. It isn't that there are some people prone to paralytic anxiety and others prone to clarifying courage. On the contrary. Recent MRI research has demonstrated that the same people who suffer from anxiety disorders have a totally normal response—in how the part of the brain known as the amygdala lights up when cued—to real danger. In other words, on United 93, the neurotics would have been right up there with everyone else in responding briskly and bravely to the clear and present threat.

The signature vexation of anxiety is that it is objectless. It washes over one in formless waves, pulls one under until the pressure and constriction are tangible and panic rears: *I'm in deep, I'm going to drown.* What is so incredibly harrowing, as the psychoanalyst Karen Horney once noted, is "the feeling of diffuseness and uncertainty, and the experience of help- lessness toward the threat."

Here is me, on my son's first-grade field trip. We are on a school bus heading to a theater to see a song-and-dance ex- travaganza about the Chinese New Year. My son and his six- year-old classmate are excitedly and mirthfully engaged in playing "I Spy," peering out the window as a drab Toronto cityscape in January drags by us in the slow, slushy traffic. These two little boys are possessed by joy. Life is marvelous. The bus smells of damp mittens and melting snow and sham- pooed hair and Juicy Fruit gum. The seats are deliciously springy. You can bounce up and down in your snow pants and not get sent into the hall. Sampling their prospects as if they were at a Sunday buffet, Geoffrey and Aidan switch from "I Spy" to snatching the hats off the boys ahead of us, and then to an imaginary Star Wars game in which they report to one another from distant parts of the galaxy, covering their mouths with their small hands and simulating static.

And I am beside them, the parent volunteer, gazing about with a feigned cheery blankness while in the grip of a name- less, indefinable angst. From the shoulders down to the hips, my body is tensely and persistently afraid. I dig my fingers into my palms as I attempt to cope with the sensation, trying to block it from my brain, my mind, my soul—to contain it as a kind of physical ache of no importance. Arthritis, a toothache, a hangover. Uncomfortable but meaningless. Let it loose from that mooring and I *am* Edvard Munch's *The Scream*. Alone, overwhelmed by dread on a happy yellow school bus filled with children.

Munch, who was plagued by it all his life, captures dread on canvas as if he were pinning a moth, an artist whose genius approached science in its precision in revealing the extent to which anxiety is both unbearably vivid yet insanely abstract. I could, I suppose, attribute my dread that day to having just read about the Doomsday Clock, or to the fact that neither my son nor his friend wore seat belts on the bus as we trundled out of the city and onto a major highway, or to the disturbingly warm winter weather, or my up-and-down bank account— the feast-to-famine existence I endure as a writer, which is ever on my mind. But why was Munch's figure screaming? What about the well-known dread of Tennyson and Yeats, of William James and Charles Darwin? Their fear went in search of a cause, I understand that. But what caused their *fear*?

"Last night the ground shook during a thunderstorm," a poster to Flu Wiki wrote, as our dark 2006 winter began to resolve into something more gently equivocal. "Today, it's spring here in Jersey. Warm, lovely. Driving, I simply couldn't hold to the belief in the pandemic, something inside said, no it can't be. I don't feel the danger, yet I do believe in what's happening intellectually. As far as feeling it, I feel like all the others I've spoken to that dismiss it. How can the mind be divided like that? Is it a right brain vs. left brain issue? Does anyone else get this duality of thought?"

This poster to the Wiki, as we all came to call it, was evincing the periodic sense of surreality that many others on this Web site felt, including me, as we attempted to do everything possible to apprehend and fend off the possibility of All of Us Dying. Unbeknownst to the fellow from Jersey, his reflections had already been beautifully articulated in 1837 by a young Danish philosopher named Søren Kierkegaard. Searingly observant and governed by his own experience of angst, the twenty-seven-year-old writer from Copenhagan offered insights into this condition that remain, in my view, unmatched by any contribution since. We think of Freud as our psychological genius, but I would argue that it's Kierkegaard. "Anxiety," he wrote, "is afraid, yet it maintains a sly intercourse with its object, cannot look away from it, indeed will not." If fear elicits action, anxiety compels obsessive contemplation: "it is a desire for what one dreads, a sympathetic antipathy. Anxiety is an alien power which lays hold of an individual, and yet one cannot tear oneself away, nor has a will to do so; for one fears, but what one fears, one desires."

Do I desire a death by avian influenza? Did the poster from New Jersey yearn to pass away in the spring rain? Certainly not. Yet we seek something. We want something, a primal sort of testing of our mettle that leads us, in the meantime, to engaging in extreme sports and sitting through movies like *Saw*. We are ready to face more profound challenges than our society appears to offer. Kierkegaard wrote, "What one desires is freedom, which is to say selfhood. We cannot mature and be fully creative by burying or displacing anxiety, but only by moving through it." Freedom isn't meant to be hedonism, so much as the actualization of purpose.

In other words, our anxiety is growing, spreading through Western culture, because we need, on a collective cultural and spiritual level, to grow. Kierkegaard called his own era "the cowardly age," in which a person "does everything possible by way of diversions and the Janizary music of loud-voiced enterprises to keep lonely thoughts away." We see that all around us now, almost two hundred years later, with the insights of existential philosophy scarcely present in the conversation anymore. Anxiety is treatable with pills, and is no longer respected as a meaningful signifier of a culture caught and flailing in arrested development.

According to data from the World Mental Health Survey, conducted in 2002 in eighteen countries, anxiety has emerged now as the most prevalent mental health problem across the globe. Yet, the incidence rates vary dramatically from nation to nation. The United States has the highest level of anxiety in the world, with a lifetime prevalence rate of 28.8 percent. By contrast, 93.4 percent of Mexicans have *never* experienced a major episode of anxiety (or depression, for that matter). An American is nine times more likely to suffer from anxiety than a resident of Shanghai, and the Germans are less anxious than the French.

This kind of data makes it strikingly obvious that anxiety is qualitatively different than fear. Want some fear? Go to Iraq, or get yourself stranded on Mount Everest. Jump out of a plane, dare to express yourself in North Korea. Be a white man on a farm in Zimbabwe.

The other day, my psychiatrist offered me his opinion that what drives anxiety in the Western world is the coveted illusion that we can be in control. Latin Americans, he argued, are bracingly accustomed to injustice and to toil and have no "fantasy" that fate is in their hands, as he put it, flipping his colorful tie back and forth and smiling at me mischievously. The Cubans and Mexicans were blasted by two powerful hurricanes in a row during the summer of 2005, and while the Americans pointed fingers and screamed at one another about who was responsible for the aftermath of Katrina, their Latin covictims just rebuilt and "kept dancing the samba," he said. He was being insouciant, but he was also being very serious. As the environmental thinker Dave Pollard has written, "This delusion of danger, and the illusion that something can or has to be done, that someone—British cows, Canadian farmers, Firestone, Saddam Hussein—must be brought to account in order to give us back control, is literally making us all crazy."

Certainly it is, because control is not what we need.

What we need is to bend to the tempest like pine and palm trees—flexible, adaptive, attuned, yet fully rooted in our principles. What we need, in essence, is to grow up.

Childhood Waves of Trust and Fear

Sleep, you black-eyed pig
Fall into a deep pit full of ghosts.
— ICELANDIC LULLABY, EARLY 19TH CENTURY

O N AN EVENING in bleak November, with the trees stripped to their skeletal frames by the chill wind, I put my daughter to bed and we talk about the world beyond her window. Sleeping by herself alarms her, so I present myself as a study in maternal calm.

"What if someone comes in and kidnaps me?" she asks, drawing her small knees up to her chin, beneath the paisley comforter on her bunk bed.

"Well, that's just not going to happen," I reply, closing her drapes. But Clara isn't a TV movie child, who accepts a sweet pep talk topped by a light kiss before drifting cheerfully into slumber. She has never cheerfully drifted. As a baby, she wouldn't surrender her sobbing and colicky consciousness without the sound of a vacuum cleaner playing on a tape cassette. She isn't, and never will be, easily reassured. My daughter is a classic example of what the Harvard child psychologist Jerome Kagan called the high reactive temperament. She was wired from birth to be quick to startle and difficult to settle. An anxious child, as I was.

"What about the girl who was taken from her house and killed in the woods?" Clara persists, throwing down this gauntlet of possibility. News has been passed around on the playground about a dark-eyed ten-year-old in our city who'd been snatched from her bed. Her remains were found in the undergrowth at the side of a bike path many months later. An acquaintance of the family pled guilty to her murder.

I wonder how to answer this. Once a crime journalist, I can handily calculate the odds—remote as lightning—that a stranger will ascend a ladder in our narrow backyard in downtown Toronto and jimmy open Clara's stiff window. Yet, I know she isn't interested in the odds. She is aware that at least one kidnapping has happened, and therefore it *might* happen again. What she is really asking me is how will she cope.

Clara's brain is still developing. While the almond-shaped amygdala in her temporal lobes, which act as the sensory headquarters of mammalian fear, can send out five-alarm panic signals, her cerebral cortex remains a work in progress, and she cannot yet rationally assess the threat and then signal back to the amygdala, "false alarm." She is terri-fied at night for the same reason that she bursts into tears several times a week during the day: she literally cannot help it. Researchers in Europe recently confirmed—no surprise to me—that parents consistently underestimate the intensity of their children's fears. It is interesting that in Western culture we send them off on their own to bed when they are least able to handle the solitude. In primates and humans, the startle reflex is potentiated by darkness. Neurologically, we have evolved to be jumpier and more hypervigilant after sunset, whereas, for example, rodents and rabbits are more wired during the day. Yet this is the only time that we actually *require* our most vulnerable members to fend for themselves. Improbably, we position them as scouts around the periphery of the campfire, then offer them no instructions beyond insisting they not sound an alarm while we slumber. "When adults try to recall their earliest fears," writes Yi-Fu Tuan in his fine book *Landscapes of Fear*, "they forget those of infancy but remember the dread of darkness."

I do indeed remember the darkness. In 1971, my family was living in New Delhi when war broke out between India and Pakistan over the fate of the newborn Bangladesh. For the two weeks leading up to Christmas that year, all householders in India's capital were told to black out their windows with paint or blinds to conceal the city from the Pakistani Air Force, which had been bombing cities farther to the north. As a child of seven, I remember terse conversations between my parents and a terrible ensuing darkness. At some point, I knelt by my bed on the cool, stone tiles and prayed that our house would not explode. One moment the walls around me were immutable and contained within them all I depended upon and loved. The next, without warning, all might be in ruins.

In the end, the only casualty in our home during the war was my small white rabbit, Marshmallow, who perished after my teenaged sister accidentally dropped him in the toilet in the inky darkness when she was getting ready for bed. "I thought the *lid* was down," she explained, full of rue.

During the three years that we lived in India, I lost weight from a combination of anxious inappetite and a distaste for mutton. The doctor prescribed a daily vanilla milk shake, which Mum bought at the American PX, the overseas grocery store that supplies U.S. diplomats and military personnel on their far-flung bases. Kraft Dinner and Aunt Jemima, Tang and frozen french fries, a treasure chest of comfort foods to covet in exotic lands. Every afternoon, I walked home from the American International School, carrying my Snoopy lunch box, holding hands with a fellow wan-faced child, the teensy pair of us evading monkeys, boys careening out of control on overladen bicycles, men on scooters, beggars, stray cows, the whole aching, solicitous world—until we parted ways at the dusty gates of my house. I would enter the cool, air-conditioned interior—the shift in temperature always shocked me—and drink my milk shake cross-legged on the floor, writing stories or watching Bollywood films on the one channel we got on our boxy TV.

India was where I populated my personal "landscape of fear," the unique psychic scenery that every person grows idiosyncratically alert to in accord with what haunted them in childhood. Psychologists would call the specificity of these responses "cued fear." One child learns to dread water because of an accident or an overly nervous parent. Another is cued to feel apprehensive about dogs. Or the desert, or dark alleys. In my case, India furnished me with a veritable parade of images. Bovine creatures, scooters, armed conflict, the inchoate prospect of getting lost or left behind—the abiding insecurity that comes with being the youngest child of world-roaming parents with much on their minds.

Predatory animals showed up during the summer that I was eight, when Sunny—the cheerful Canadian High Commission driver—ferried us north to the old English hill station of Bhimtal in the foothills of the Eastern Himalayas. This was a high alpine valley with a glacial lake near Corbett National Park, the habitat of India's famed man-eating tigers. We were headed for a lodge owned by an adventuresome Czech named Mr. Smetacek, who had a vast and mysterious collection of pinned butterflies.

The trip was to be a lulling respite for two intensely stressed adults, three extremely stirred-up teenagers living out the Woodstock gestalt in the very country that invented the symbols of hippiedom, and me—whatever I was. Small and tag-along, I rode, as was my custom, in the farthest back of our cherry red station wagon, gazing out the grimed rear window as the ill-paved road receded along the dusty flatlands that ringed Delhi, watching women struggle along with what seemed like entire haystacks on their bent backs, their strange humped figures dwindling into a sheen of heat as we sped onward over the burning asphalt.

After hours of car sickness and sibling bickering, we reached the foothills and began to traverse the narrow switchback road that zigzagged upward thousands of feet through prime bus-plunge territory to the turnoff above Bhimtal.

There comes a time in every fraught family road trip— my mother can't remember exactly what the trigger was that night, though she thinks Sunny got lost, missed a turn, perhaps Dad snapped at him—when everyone suddenly barks "damn you, no damn *you*, damn it all to hell." At that moment on this trip, my generally even-tempered mother demanded to be let out of the station wagon. She wasn't thinking. "It was just—" she says to me now, "it was the *tension* in that car. I couldn't stand it." Consumed by this need to escape, she got out, extracted me—whom she wore habitually around her neck "like a boa," as she likes to say—and waved off our ride. With the wagon's red taillights winking up ahead like tiger's eyes until they flickered out of view, the two of us began to walk. Walk where? "I thought it was a matter of yards," she admits to me now, "perhaps a hundred yards."

Instead, in the uncanny pitch-black world, with the moonlight trapped by an overcast sky and no polluting urban light for hundreds of miles, in a dark so profound that we needed a flashlight to follow the road but had none, my mother and I trudged on for half a mile. It was July, just before the monsoon, a time of year when the farmers set deliberate brush fires on the mountain slopes. And so we found ourselves moving tentatively ahead through a darkness punctuated unpredictably by crackling bursts of orange flame. Hansel and Gretel. Frodo and Sam. A mythic sense of what it means to move one foot ahead of the next. "The whole hill was on fire, below us and above us," my mother recalls. At length, we found the others at the lodge, milling about in a fright, for Mr. Smetacek had greeted them with news that a mountain lion had been seen prowling the area that night. We unpacked our belongings in spooked silence and went to bed. My memory of our vacation from there on in, those fragments of recollection that stay with me, have to do with being newly attuned to the prospect of danger. I remember playing by myself along a low stone wall, imagining myself a ballerina, balancing and spinning and yet also alert—on the lookout for rustlings in the bushes. Peaceful and tense all at once, like a deer.

For years, until high school at least, I felt—was consumed by—an indefinable sense of responsibility in the darkness. I had to be on the lookout. I *had* to be. When we returned from India and took up residence in a huge old wooden house in Ottawa, I fended off sleep to stand guard at the portal of darkness for what seemed half the night. The Ottawa house was rambling and magical for a child, filled with nooks and crannies and slidable banisters and a wraparound, gabled veranda. The walls creaked. The basement was rough and cold. Painted white and set back in a big yard on a quiet street, it resembled the pretty residence in *The Amityville Horror*. As the youngest of five children, I was assigned the former sewing room, a little space that faced the wide staircase leading to the third floor. Beyond my doorway, halls receded every which way into the fathomless gloom.

Every night, in the process of surveilling the stairs, I was obliged to turn my back on the window, against which my slender bed was pressed. This was like an open invitation to the werewolf . . . or tiger . . . or Hillside Strangler out there on the balcony to sneak up and shock me with his unbidden presence. What I was afraid of, I think, was the prospect of being badly frightened; all this silence and darkness felt like the vulnerable tension on the surface of water. One fist through it, one shout or flare of light would change everything, utterly. You see how the original scenario, which was the Indo-Pakistani War, had receded from my child memory and been replaced by whatever came presently to mind, such as news just then on television about serial killers in Los Angeles, while the formative *emotional* sketch or template remained. The night terrified me, but I had forgotten why. My fear went in search of new causes.

The best option for monitoring the house was to lie face to the ceiling, swiveling my head back and forth from doorway to window until my hair grew hopelessly mussed and my flannel nightie tangled. A breakthrough came when my mother bought me a candy-colored portable radio, and I could distract myself by whispering along to the Carpenters or the Captain & Tennille. "We've only just begun," I'd sing beneath the blanket, "to live . . ." What would I have done without Karen?

It is possible that, at that point, I had developed what neuropsychiatrists call "anxiety sensitivity." Adults with panic disorder and agoraphobia are governed mostly by the apprehension of the panic attack itself, that they will panic without warning and won't be able to cope. They cannot predict it; that is what haunts them and keeps them out of restaurants and subways. "Fear came upon me," Henry James Sr. wrote in a letter to his son William, and "the thing had not lasted ten seconds before I felt myself a wreck: that is, reduced from a state of firm, vigourous, joyful manhood to one of almost helpless infancy." So sudden and extreme is this experience that it is like being punched in the face.

The god Pan was aptly imagined by the Greeks as a metaphor for the ancient human conundrum of panic. The irritable goat-man was said to despise having his naps interrupted and would leap out unexpectedly at noisy travelers, roaring terribly in a rage and filling them instantly with terror. Interestingly, Pan never did actual harm, for he carried no weapon. His power to scare lay entirely in his unanticipated appearance. The Greeks wrote little of enduring analytical value about the psychology of fear and anxiety, but they nailed panic (and coined it) through this projection.

Anxiety sensitivity is thought to be a significant harbinger, in children, for the later development of an anxiety disorder.

So is an intense fear of the dark due to enhanced (or too-easily elicited) startle reflex. Both are more important indicators of adult proneness than specific phobias, or anxieties about death or separation. In other words, a child who is hellishly afraid of snakes but relatively easy to tuck into bed is less likely to be anxious in adulthood than a child who charges about the daytime landscape quite fearlessly, then falls apart at night.

Mornings were glorious in my childhood, for I could rejoin the exciting business of living, released from my loneliness and struggle by early sunlight and the welcoming fragrance of breakfast. By day, I was fearless. I would jump off the garage roof in the ludicrous hope that I could break my leg and wear a cast for everyone at school to sign. In every arena I was gregarious, outgoing, adventurous. When I felt nervous in daylight, what I generally experienced was the healthy and bracing anxiety—before a gymnastics meet or up on the school stage—that Freud called "anxious readiness" and that Kierkegaard described as "the alarming possibility of being able." The clear and heightened moment before we leap from the rocks to the river below.

The necessary summoning of the senses that propels us forward and enables our growth.

There is another ordinary childhood fear we all contend with—what German philosophers once described as *Urangst*. An American slave lullaby sums it up fairly succinctly: "Hush lil' baby, don' yo' cry / Fadder an' mudder born to die." Most children, upon making the astonishing discovery at around five that their parents are mortal, manage to find their way through the awareness of human contingency without being stopped in their tracks. What assists them are nursery songs and fairy tales, but in an unexpected manner. The most enduringly popular narratives for children do not soothe their fears by denying them, but in fact, by acknowledging their existence.

As a new mother, I was struck by the foreboding in the half-remembered songs I sang to Clara; I didn't know what to make of them. "When the bough breaks, the cradle will fall / And down will come baby, cradle and all." A threat of disaster contained in a crooning melody? The cultural historian Marina Warner explains the ambiguous and faintly menacing content of lullabies quite brilliantly: "In this recurrent formula, prophetic ironies work a kind of sorrowful magic: the lullaby as future personal narrative opens into a universal commentary on the frailty of human life." We engage our children in their own rendition of the blues, and they draw consolation—the way we do—from the admixture of lilting tune and ain't-it-true lyric poignancy.

Fairy tales serve a similar function. As Bruno Bettelheim first pointed out, a recurrent theme in the stories of Charles Perrault and the Brothers Grimm is the dark forest, the lost path, the dead or abandoning parents, all reflective of children's interior sense of psychic danger. Notes Tuan in *Landscapes of Fear*, "The fairy tale frankly describes the bad experiences that children know to be an intimate part of their lives but that adults seldom acknowledge. It shows the young that pain is necessary to growth, that one must pass through distressing thresholds to a higher state of being."

"Nothing will happen to you, sweetie," I often tell my daughter as I smooth her honey-colored hair against her forehead. But she knows better; she has read the Brothers Grimm.

The gifting to children of a subtle and complex series of stories and songs that help them wrestle with fear appears to have been entirely unconscious—an oeuvre of intuitive genius brought to us by the nursemaids and mothers who are credited as "Anon." Two hundred years ago, a child such as Clara might have struggled with the specter of the bogeyman, or in Germany, the erlking, or in Russia, the baby-gobbling witch Baba Yaga, who lurked and hungered in her creepy, chicken-legged house. What if, *what if?* a child might fret. And the parent or nurse would have countered with the dangers of staying awake, raising the idea of the sandman, who hunted through the night for watchful children and threw handfuls of sand in their wide-open eyes—"until they are bloodied," as one nursery rhyme goes. In rural Egypt, the threat took the form of being eaten alive by the *silowa*; in Kenya, by the prowling *manani*. In our time, we think we've relinquished the nonsense of monsters. But they remain within our society, and children see them. The erlking has been supplanted by the pedophile, the fable by the headline.

The National Institute of Mental Health reports that 13 percent of American children suffer from anxiety disorders in any given six-month period. Given that this refers to disordered anxiety, as opposed to developmentally typical childhood fears, the statistic is surprisingly high. One would more likely expect to find it in a war zone (as one does) than in a peaceful and affluent nation. One thing anxious children lack in this culture that has traditionally been granted to them is what psychologists call a "recipe" for dealing with their dread. What is meant by this is a ritual or a prayer. An *action* that can be undertaken to offset the almost unendurable feeling of helplessness that characterizes anxiety. When an English nanny warned her charges: "If you don't behave, the bogeyman will get you," she was nevertheless offering an option. Behave in a particular way, and you'll be fine. That is what is meant by a recipe. Whereas now, in a good-hearted and entirely unintentional manner, we set our anxious children up for sleepless nights by simply denying that there's anything to be anxious about in the darkness, and therefore inadvertently implying that there's nothing that can be done. When we say "there's nothing to worry about," what the very worried and imaginative child hears is "we are unaware of the danger so you must redouble your vigilance. You're on your own, kid: we don't *see* dead people." When Clara asks me "what if?" she is seeking a recipe. A way to cope. What is lost in supplanting the fable with the headline is this matter of *knowing what to do*.

Experimentally, I offer my daughter a strategy. I say, "Okay, let's talk about what you can do if an intruder breaks in. There *are* things you can do. Let's make a list to tack to your wall that shows you steps you can take to protect yourself. Number one: you can yell. Did you know that the very few children who have had strangers come into their rooms may not have thought to yell? They obeyed the kidnapper's command to be quiet. They didn't wake up their parents! And guess what? Strangers who sneak into bedrooms are terribly nervous themselves. They know it's wrong, and that they might get caught. You can scare them off! This is one of life's rules to remember, Clara. You are not the only one who is scared."

Over the next few days, Clara gets caught up in the imaginative task of devising ingenious ways to foil robbers. She has a miniature flashlight from a birthday party loot bag that she will beam into a robber's eyes. She builds a rattle out of pennies and a tin can, meant to startle the robber. She makes plans to pop a balloon in his face. She devises a sort of robber baffle for her windowsill, with rocks and pointy tacks and cleverly tied string.

I don't interject with my own views about what would deter an intruder. The point of the exercise is purely psychological. Clara begins to see that she is resourceful, and this revelation seems to empower her. The anxiety begins to ebb. It's an amazing thing to watch. "From this moment on," as the novelist Count Villiers de L'Isle-Adam wrote of his nine-year-old heroine in *Isis*, "what was dreaming confusedly in the eyes of this little girl took on a more fixed glint: one would have said she was feeling the meaning of herself while awakening in our shadows."

I cannot tell, yet, whether Clara is merely a "worrier," in

the fashion of my mother, whose lively intelligence literally wakes her up at night and casts her into problem-solving mode, or whether my daughter will grow up to experience the full-blown "generalized anxiety disorder" that has plagued me in adulthood. The research (particularly in twin studies) suggest that children of parents with an anxiety disorder are considerably more likely to show "anxiety proneness," through a blend of inherited genes and learned fear. Consider the anxious parent who urges her child to "get away from the edge of the dock!" If her child grows apprehensive about water or the prospect of tumbling off edges, then theoretically the parent will have conveyed about a third of that fearfulness through genetics, and another two-thirds through her own behavior.

If I examine my family tree, feeling for the tense and brittle branches, I find myself tracing my father's line, through his mother, and beyond to her family in the Canadian prairie town of Winnipeg: the Moodys. How mordantly appropriate. My great-grandmother, I am told, was such a "stern" woman that she refused to allow Granny to marry until Great-Aunt Grace, the elder sister, was also engaged—and then they had to marry on the same day. The head nurse at Winnipeg General Hospital, who gave birth to her first child after forty, she was known to be critical and intolerant, seeing no need to indulge the whims of youth. "Sharp tongued," as my aunt recalls. This is not proof that my great-grandmother was depressive or anxious, rather than quick to funnel her mood into causing other people arbitrary misery. But I have seen echoes of her in my paternal grandmother, the beautiful and quick-witted Maryon Moody, destined to become Canada's first lady, to dine at state dinners with the Kennedys and Johnsons and Queen Elizabeth. In her private diaries, she often wrote tartly about these encounters, noting her upset that LBJ's helicopters had whirled above her garden and blown her flowers away; remarking that the wife of Indian Prime Minister Nehru "dressed like an unmade bed." She was, in essence, irritable.

Granny grew famous in Canada for her acerbic remarks on the campaign trail. When my affable grandfather Lester B. Pearson gave a stump speech as prime minister and then, returning to her side, asked if he'd missed anything important, she replied within earshot of reporters, "Yes, several opportunities to sit down." I think of her as the only first lady in world history who worshipped at the altar of Dorothy Parker. She literally did, quoting Parker to journalists: "Behind every successful man stands a surprised woman." I suspect she glimpsed in Parker a similar sense of aghast dismay at the world. "Mixed anxiety and depression," my psychiatrist would likely jot down if he evaluated Granny today.

As she aged, she grew more fractious, and went about everywhere with a menthol cigarette and a cutting remark. But it wasn't toughness she projected; she seemed more like a woman concealing pain. At length her mind began to cloud over, and she was reduced to simple neediness. She phoned our house a dozen times a day.

As I write, I'm staying with my father—her son—in Ottawa, in early April, where the skies are gray and the earth just faintly green. A sullen promise of spring, reluctant still. A cold rain falls all day. It reminds me of Ireland, where I once followed Dad to the grave of W. B. Yeats, one of his favorite poets. We stood near the tombstone beneath our black umbrellas, and he gazed admiringly at the epitaph: "Cast a cold eye on life, on death. Horseman pass by." He wasn't aware that Yeats suffered from anxiety. For my seventy-nine-year-old father, the label would be modern babble. Unacceptable. But he relates profoundly to the poet, and also to T. S. Eliot, for whom melancholy was a bitter friend and muse.

My father paces his kitchen, dressed in flannels and sports jacket, his shirt buttoned up to the throat, his major relinquishment to life in retirement being the absence of a tie. I sit at the breakfast table reading the paper—alarm, alarm, blah-blah this and oh, horror that—while he tries to fix the day's logistics in his mind.

"So, you're going out, are you?" he asks for the fifth time.

"Yes, at one o'clock," I murmur, not lifting my eyes from the news.

"And who are you going to see?" he asks, with a slight uptick to his voice, as if merely wishing to be reminded.

"A friend. A colleague."

"At one, you say?"

"Yes."

He paces some more, from window to stove, his breathing a touch shallow, his ample white hair a little disheveled from running his hands through. His movements are still fluid and graceful. He was once a fabulous dancer. I remember joining him on the floor during a cruise down the river Neva, when he was Canada's ambassador to Moscow; how game he was to find the rhythm in a Donna Summer song. He was also a fabled quipster, a dry accoutrement to any diplomatic dinner party in the manner of Oscar Wilde. A heckler. A man of bons mots. He was a fine historian, a beautiful writer, a skilled diplomat. Now, he just wants to get one thing straight:

"So, you're going out, are you?"

I nod, and we travel the route again. Where are you going/when are you going/why are you going?

I would write it down, but he's not interested in consulting a note. The ritual of what he's doing—the obsessive-compulsive nature of the exercise—entails his inquiring aloud and being answered. He needs it straight across the room from my mouth to his ear. Each time, he gives a brief nod.

At noon, while I'm nursing my third cup of coffee, he pours himself a small glass of wine: another ritual, one that began when the checking on logistics set in—after he drove off one morning in his Honda to meet a friend for golf and found himself unfathomably lost. The experience marked his first awareness of the memory loss that is edging, very subtly and slowly, in upon him. It was such a shock—so haunting—to get "turned around" on this road he habitually traveled that he grew white-knuckled and tense there and then, and has been waging a silent battle to regain composure ever since.

Before my one o'clock appointment, we go for a walk, on level ground, past the valiant daffodils fighting to bloom in the rain. Toward the end of the block he gets winded. He stops speaking in midsentence, unable to catch his breath. This alarms me. Is it heart trouble? But he's been checked, he's had an EKG. It occurs to me that he's having a panic attack.

I tell him so, and he won't hear of it. As ridiculous a suggestion as my saying he's been cursed by a witch. He waves his hand as if I were a teenaged goth promoting faddish notions and mutters "certainly not." I stand there in all my naïve finery, in my childish costume, making absurd proclamations, when he, my father, was an ambassador during the Cold War. I can hardly press my point. This is a man who was packed off to boarding school at the age of nine, separated from his parents by the Atlantic Ocean during World War II and made to withstand the singing smack of the rod on his legs while his mother and father endured the London Blitz. That was the way of things, the nature of living through history. What does *personal* anxiety have to with anything important?

All this, by way of retort, he contains within the single gesture of waving his hand. I can easily make his argument for him, because it's interwoven with the story of his life, within our family recollections and whispered confidences, our photographs and letters, even my grandfather's published memoirs. (Lester B. trips lightly over his days at Gallipoli during World War I, even though it infused him with the passion that would eventually win him a Nobel Peace Prize. He notes only, reaching for the absurdity, that he got out of there by winning a baseball tourney, and then escaped the rest of the war entirely by being struck by a London bus.) We are an Anglo-Irish folk for whom fear has two remedies: black humor and teeth-clenching grit. In university, my father, an otherwise deeply contemplative and serious man, was nicknamed "the Joker."

Now he shows angst plainly in the cool, ambivalent light of Canada in April, and I want to say, "Dad, I know this. It's bred in the bone. Your terrors are my terrors." But we're like two souls on either side of an iron bridge, with history and culture and gender rushing between us. A great, roaring river. He strains a little, he cocks his ear, he yearns for the answering human voice caught up and distorted by the rush of the water. But he cannot hear me. Horseman, pass by.

Sometimes, in considering how I wandered out of childhood only to fall into a deep pit full of ghosts in my late teens and twenties, collapsing three times, by my own rough count, into psychiatric "disorder," I wonder if this familial legacy of rectitude didn't combine, entirely by accident, with the new and more combustible history of my own time. What I mean, as I hope you will see, is that I didn't think to protest or question my predicament in relation to my times any more than my father did. I took it on the chin, like I'd been taught. Only, what I took on the chin was something altogether more ambiguous and confusing than war. It was love.

3

Class Notes on a
Nervous Breakdown

I was run over by the truth one day.
Ever since the accident I've walked this way.

—ADRIAN MITCHELL

I N THE SUMMER of 1987, Paul Simon's *Graceland* was on the radio, making waves.

"Somebody could walk into this room right now and say your life is on fire," he sang, and I hummed along, going about the teeth-clenched business of appearing cheerful and competent even though my life was, in fact, on fire. Others could say it, that my existence appeared to be aflame, but they wouldn't. Somebody—anybody?—could mention that curious development about my life, but nobody did. What qualified as a fire in one's life, in the Western world in 1987? Obviously, if you were run over by a truck or lost all your savings to a swindler or got diagnosed with grave illness, that counted and qualified. But if the man you were deeply in love with essentially tipped you out of the window of your shared home in a happy spirit of spring-cleaning, like you were so much clutter, that was just ordinary, late-twentieth-century life, and I was my father's daughter. Tough out history, don't complain.

This is how I came to be diagnosed with "generalized anxiety disorder" when I was twenty-three. I had a nervous breakdown while on scholarship at the University of Chicago's graduate school because I had neither the will nor the permission to call a halt to my affairs, to request a time-out of a month or two, to wave my arms in the air and shout "Whoa, whoa, whoa. What the hell just happened *to my life*?" The world I had been living in with a wild, committed ardor had totally and suddenly collapsed, and nobody had observed the explosion but me.

The details are so typical of my generation that they're almost embarrassing to relay. I had been living for a year with a man I loved as fiercely as Heloise loved Abelard. We shared the top two floors of a small Victorian house belonging to an Italian family in downtown Toronto. I made him chicken with white wine and grapes, a recipe I copied carefully from *The Silver Palate Cookbook*, and his swooning reaction was like a diamond ring, a fur coat. He made love to me against the bathroom wall minutes after I came home from my job. In our bedroom, in a church yard, on a beach, in the shadows of alleys on the way home from the theater. He said, "I'll always love you." I felt so alive that my skin burned. My back arched like a cat when he touched me.

I remember everything from that year, the way that the leaves spiced the road on October evenings, how the air tingled in January, so sharp and clear; the translucent blue of a nordic spring sky. The world was suffused with sweetness; it had a musical clarity. Everything felt true. But it wasn't. The hammer fell at my family's old wooden lake house, built a century earlier by my great-grandfather with an A-frame vision and some nails jutting out of his mouth. On an August evening redolent with the smell of dead weasel, the man I hoped to marry announced in happy pleasure that he'd discovered it was possible to love me and a woman named Poppy at the same time. He was relaxing his handsome six-foot frame on the saggy old porch bed and showing not a trace of discomfort when he said this. With his smooth mood and contented demeanor, he was conveying that he couldn't care less if I fell down a well. All other things being equal, there'd be Poppy. And after her, a further delicious sampling, presumably, of Heathers and Suzannes.

It is difficult to describe the shock of this unmasking. In one conversation, he had managed to crush everything I understood to be real. Is love real? What about trust? Was the last year of my life an authentic experience? Is *he* real? I suspect the location had something to do with the depth of my horror. My cottage was my stronghold, a place with affectionate ghosts and fond memories and century-old books and a banner painted over the fireplace by my grandmother: "Fra ghosties and ghoulies and long-leggedy beasties, may the guid lord deliver us." Here on my intimate turf, my life partner unraveled our prospects as casually as a man yawning and flinging down his cards in a poker game. "Well, I'm done."

Shortly after, he advised me with the most earnest of intentions that I would make someone "a wonderful wife and mother someday." Just not him.

And that was it, I was transformed into the screaming figure on Edvard Munch's bridge. *Mouth slack, eyes melting, body a vibrating wail.* This was about the time that Tina Turner was belting out "What's love got to do with it?" in a saucy black dress on brand-new MTV, and those of us who were parented by a generation who felt that love, actually, had lots to do with it were completely unprepared for the tectonic shift in values. Need I tell you the following: love is a scarce and inestimable treasure that is appalling to lose. That is rudimentary human wisdom, the stuff of every civilization's literature and poetry and psalms for thousands of years; but when I was twenty-three, it was a notion bent to the guillotine, its trappings of commitment, loyalty, and constructive partnership deemed to be dangerous artifacts of an ancien régime.

Stunned and heartbroken, but well-schooled in stoicism by my Protestant parents, I set off for graduate school on Chicago's South Side during the height of the crack epidemic. Some would say that this wasn't a suitably calming environment; for me, it felt entirely appropriate. Gunfire, sirens, boom boxes, incomprehensible conversation in seminars about the methodology of the historian Michel Foucault. Everywhere, a discordant and alarming strangeness. I had but one objective: to make sense of what had just happened in my life. If I could make sense of it, I could regain a modicum of control over my fate. That wasn't a conscious, articulated goal. It was something more akin to a nervous tic. Invited to another new graduate student's cocktail party on a Friday night, I more or less had to reply, "Thanks, Amy, I really hope to make that—but one proviso: I have to figure out, first, why the love of my life just transmogrified before my eyes into an alert yet indifferent insect."

Maria Miceli has noted, "Without a certain degree of stability and reliability of one's model of the world, including oneself, one faces the threat of succumbing to a serious destabilization of either one's conceptual system or personality structure."

Yes, one does! Floridly destabilized, floundering around like a hog on ice. More than fifty years ago, the psychologist Rollo May, drawing on and refining the insights of such thinkers as Karen Horney, Eric Erikson, and Kurt Goldstein, proposed that pathological anxiety was "cued off by a threat to some value that the individual holds essential to his existence as a personality." Rollo May had many long conversations with the great German theologian Paul Tillich, who resided in his waning days in Chicago. Tillich was much taken up with the existentialist's concept of the dread of "non-being." This wasn't an anxiety about death, so much as an abiding sense of unease about possessing neither purpose nor impact. Of failing to *be* in the world. I think of it as the dream in which you scream but make no sound, or run but make no progress. Write your name in the sand; watch it erased by the waves. This is non-being. May brought the existentialist perspective to his clinical work as a psychologist in New York, and observed that in some cases, extreme anxiety entails a kind of disintegration of one's core perspective. It "may consist of the loss of psychological or spiritual meaning which is identified with one's existence as a self, ie, the threat of meaninglessness."

What defines your meaning? What is your outline, what are your markers, what confirms your significance? (Asks a young, know-nothing woman: Am I not pretty enough, am I not sexy enough, am I not smart enough? What am I not? What am I failing to be? Why have you *left* me? Why didn't I make a mark on your soul?)

Research shows that anxiety amid college students is extremely high right now, with about 35 percent of students seeking treatment from their campus mental health centers, according to the Anxiety Disorders Association of America. The psychologist Jean Twenge, of the University of California, San Diego, did a comparative analysis of mental health in the United States in the 1950s and 1990s, and reported that "anxiety increased so much (in this time) that the average college student in the 1990s was more anxious than 85 percent of students in the 1950s." Some of this self-doubt has to do with intensified standards for success, about which much has been written of late. (When I applied for university in 1980, no one could care less if I owned a pair of running shoes or had ever candy-striped; I did a face-plant into the 35th percentile for math on my GRE and still got a scholarship. Weren't those the days.) Nevertheless, clawing at impossible levels of status remains the goal of relatively few.

Not everyone aims to get into Harvard, but virtually everyone hopes to fall in love.

Several studies have unearthed the unsurprising fact that "problems in intimate relationships are among those reported most frequently by college students." The quest for elite achievement is not the uppermost struggle for most students; rather it is the quest for meaningful attachment. Among college seniors in one study, of the 62 percent who had broken up with a lover that year, nearly 40 percent reported feeling "anxiety about something or someone almost all of the time."

This is remarkable, considering the sexual insouciance of the generation that tails mine, with their Ivy League "naked parties" and proud declarations about the liberating efficiency of spurning romance in favor of hooking up. One wonders with what result, if not a spike in the rates of anxiety, depression, and suicide. Consider the developmental psychologist Eric Erikson's theory, that the decade of one's twenties is a time when forming intimate relationships beyond one's original family is an essential psychic drive. The need to do more than deliver blow jobs, in Erikson's view, is as developmentally critical to psychological growth as going through the "terrible twos," or enacting one's teen rebellion. Evolutionary psychologists, more reductively, might call it the drive toward "pair-bonding." However it's framed, we need—we are compelled—to build relationships in early adulthood. The great social upheavals of the twentieth century, in liberating love from sex, and sex from procreation, left no instructions about how to weave new meaning into this most elemental experience. We find ourselves staggering beneath the weightlessness of things.

Visit the discussion forums on, for example, the Quarter-life Crisis Web site, where twenty-somethings chat about their loneliness and struggle. What you'll find are lost young men and women who are so bereft of a vocabulary of meaning that they post their questions with embarrassed uncertainty: "I'm still kind of haunted by my breakup," one person posted, "but it's been, like, six months. Shouldn't I be over it by now?" Their impoverished expectations for themselves—for what should matter—appears to be the echoing dénouement of that long-ago Summer of Love. Freedom has devolved into something less exalted, and altogether more haunting.

While I went about the business of settling into Chicago, making friends, attending courses, and going to movies and museums, I never, for a moment, ceased to think about this man I loved. About my relationship to this man, and what I might have done to lose him. How did I lose him? How did I misunderstand our connection? How did a love so vivid and hopeful just vanish? What *is* love? Trying to gain traction through fierce analysis, I wound up in an obsessive-compulsive groove. It didn't involve checking taps or washing hands, so much as revisiting—as repetitively as my father asking me the time—the contours of my love affair. I have since heard this described as "retroactive anxiety," featuring "intrusive thoughts." What'd I do?/what'd I do?/what'd I do?/who

is he?/who am I?/who is he?/who am I?/what'd I do?/what
can I do? *What can I do?*

Had I been living in a village, an elder would have been a
good person to consult at this point. A mentor, a shaman, a
priest. But I was at a huge American graduate school among
strangers consumed by their studies, my family distant and my
understanding of the crisis remote. Left to my own devices, I
tried to solve the equation as if it were math. If q equals b,
then c is π^2. Aah.

During breaks in one seminar held in the Regenstein Library, I would steal over to the poetry stacks and thumb
through volumes by Emily Dickinson and Yeats, seeking an
articulation of my experience—as if the need to make sense
of it were as powerful as unwatered thirst.

*"Turning and turning in the widening gyre / The falcon cannot
hear the falconer."*

I listened to Peter Gabriel in my Walkman as I paced back
and forth along the University of Chicago's slim midway, a
stretch of brown grass between two roads that abutted the
turbulent great lake, marking the border between Leo Strauss's
realm of fierce philosophy on the north side, and the chaos
of the drug-infested ghetto to the south. Litter and rhetoric
and heartbreak, gunfire and desolate wind. Isolation, mostly.
My companions were cigarettes. Years later, a friend who is a
dedicated diarist told me that I'd confided to him, at some
point that autumn in a letter, that I'd begun feeling a kind of
panic; it was beginning to appear in my daily life, and it

was—so noted my friend, quoting me—"a panic that you could not show."

In January, I visited the student medical center. I wanted to ask the earnest young psychiatric resident who met me in a small plain room if I was losing my mind, but I couldn't seem to convey the urgency. Before the advent of antidepressants, you could walk into the office of a mental health counselor looking like an electrified cat, and they'd ask you to sit down and talk about your relationship with your mother. The conversation was not helpful. My interest wasn't *idle*. I sat curled in a tight fetal ball on his chair, too confounded to explain in a coherent way that I woke up each day thinking about this man and fell asleep with the same circular monologue in my head. I had grown paralyzed by the simplest decisions: I would stare at the phone in my dorm room for up to an hour, trying to will myself to call the library or the bank, or whatever the task at hand was. I couldn't concentrate on newspaper headlines, much less the demanding texts of my graduate work.

A point came when nothing was frightening because everything was, and I felt a certain kind of bra-ha-ha joy. Like a character in a Stephen King novel who suddenly laughs hysterically after all of her friends' heads have exploded. I began hanging out at a South Side blues club called the Checkerboard Lounge. One night, in the stark darkness of a Chicago winter, I danced without escort or inhibition, eliciting amused comments from the singer, Junior Wells, who wore a brown velour fedora. He grinned, and I smiled, and you could smell the steaming wool of coats and the tang of bourbon and the sour barley of beer, and I've rarely felt so alive. I was naïve and dismantled and vital. Purely reactive, surrendered. Moving to the blues on that scuffed vinyl floor, I was caught up in an implicitly sympathetic community, for whom music was both lament and consolation.

For a time, during these evenings at the Checkerboard, I was connecting to an essential human tradition of ameliorating personal sorrow through communal ritual. The deep comfort you draw from being swept up in some joined purpose or exaltation, in a chorus, a protest, a dance—of knowing that you're not alone. But these evenings were scarce. Usually, I could be found at the library or in my dorm room, sometimes hearing on the phone from A., who seemed to need to reassure himself, periodically, that I still loved him, or wasn't "too mad." Just to square away his conscience or take another bite of the treat or who knows what, he slept with me during my Christmas break, shattering my sense of reality all over again. I was a fool in my hoping. Maybe we all were. Afterward, I phoned the high school sweetheart whom I'd broken up with during my undergraduate days. "I'm sorry," I told him. "I'm sorry I did that."

In February 1988, as Harold Bloom published his new interpretation of his Chicago friend Saul Bellow's *Herzog*, I flew to Boston to consult papers in the archives at Harvard for my master's thesis. The trouble was that I couldn't seem to make it from my room at the B and B to Harvard's campus a few blocks away. Instead, I wound up at a coffee shop en route, there to grab breakfast, but unable to leave for the rest of the day. My experience of "intrusive thinking" was turning me into a broken machine.

In my inability to put this total body blow of emotional meaninglessness to rest, I had simply come to a halt. Kierkegaard described this as getting caught, or "shut in." In a room without windows or doors. In solitary confinement, concealed in plain view. I phoned my mother from a pay phone near Boston's Au Bon Pain on a wintry afternoon, stamping at the cold in my cowboy boots. "I need to come home," I said, having no idea how to explain what I meant. She knew. She hadn't said anything at Christmas, when I'd been found standing in a paralytic stupor in a mall by an old friend, literally unable to select and buy gifts. Since then, she'd been going about her day with one ear cocked, the way mothers do. Chicago's academic rules forbade those on scholarship from skipping a semester, so I skipped out of Chicago completely.

I landed in my elder sister's warm, calm home in the town of Dundas, Ontario, where I had been invited to stay. A psychiatrist had been arranged, but he couldn't see me for six weeks. I'm not sure why it is that people who suffer depressive breakdowns can check at once into hospitals, as can celebrities suffering from "exhaustion," whereas people afflicted by anxious breakdowns are left to carry on, to float, to depersonalize, until—as in my case—they gradually get so disoriented that they feel alienated from their own feet. "[Anxiety] is cosmic, in that it invades us totally, penetrating our whole subjective universe," noted May. Once I lost my confidence in judging what was real, it was bound to follow relatively soon thereafter that I couldn't be entirely sure of my feet.

It was Easter before the phone rang through from McMaster-Chedoke medical center. I was standing in my sister's kitchen musing, "How can these feet things be of me?" when I was summoned, at last, by Dr. X. I remember little of this first psychiatrist, except that he was square-shouldered, white-haired, and aloof. He evinced not the faintest interest in my life story. Who was I, if not an assem-blage of brain neurons that had walked into his office clothed in Levi's? He declared that "a switch had been tripped" in my brain that needed "resetting." Unlike healthy people, he explained, I was possessed of a brain that couldn't stop issuing chemical alarm signals once it had started. My head, for all intents and purposes, was behaving like a de-mented car siren. All it needed, Dr. X advised, was a firm, shut-up thwack in the guise of potent chemicals. These took the form of a prescription for lithium. He sent me off with a square of paper and a new sense of self. I was no longer a heartbroken young woman alive in a disorienting time. I was a disordered person with a wonky brain. I had "generalized anxiety disorder." There was nothing wrong with my world. What was wrong, and fixable with chemicals, was me.

The notion that anxiety was a brain disorder would have mystified my Scottish ancestors, who sought protection fra ghosties and ghoulies from God. There was no awareness of anxiety as a category of illness—as opposed to the normal state of affairs—prior to the rise of office-based psychiatry in the twentieth century. In Greek mythology, according to the Athens psychiatrist Yiannis Papakostas, gods were the embodiment of madness. Hecate, a lunar goddess, was believed to cause epileptic insanity, Dionysus triggered elation, Diana stirred hysteria, and Pan created fear. This accepted idea was carried through into Christianity via the notion that various distresses were caused by sin or a crowd of saints and Devils. "The Lord shall smite thee with madness, and blindness, and astonishment of heart." King David, who famously fought Goliath about 3,525 years ago, was abundantly troubled in his old age; he is reported in the Bible as saying that his "soul was alarmed," and that "fearfulness and trembling are come upon me." Recently, a pair of psychiatrists undertook a retroactive analysis of David, much like the one done on Abraham Lincoln a few years ago, and concluded that he was likely suffering from clinical depression. But David wouldn't have construed it that way, and arguably the way that he did construe it—*my soul is alarmed*—was more meaningful, both to him and to us.

By the tenth century, Christendom had a patron saint for those suffering from "la panique" and "les frayeures," a certain St. Gilles of France. This suggests that people were seeking relief specifically from the grip of fear. But whether the fear they wanted eased was proportionate to the hazard of their lives, or more diffuse and irrational, is impossible to guess.

By the eighteenth century, psychiatrists (or alienists, as they were then known) presided over the major mental illnesses in remote asylums, while everybody else just carried on with the business of plague, war, dying in childbirth, starving, and so on without consulting an expert. If you were awash in nameless dread, you might avail yourself of opium—which many people did, popping a few grains at bedtime the way we now consume the sleeping pill Ambien—or they might swallow a tablet of chloral hydrate, some bromine, maybe drink ale or port, or engage in fervent prayer.

In the asylums, the alienists tended to neurosyphilis, schizophrenia, psychosis, paranoia, and manic depression, although they wouldn't have recognized those labels, and mostly had no idea what they were doing beyond warehousing the unmanageably insane. Until the German clinician Emil Kraepelin came up with the classifications we still use, in his carefully systemized files at the end of the nineteenth century, the mentally ill were assigned a rather poetic hodgepodge of diagnoses: "masturbatory insanity," "moon madness," "wedding-night psychosis," "old maid's insanity," to name a few cited by Edward Shorter in his superb *A History of Psychiatry*.

The first medical description of anxiety (that I've been able to find, at any rate) appears in a 1733 book penned by the physician George Cheyne, called *The English Malady: or a treatise of nervous disorders of all kinds, as spleen, vapours, lowness of spirits, hypochondrial and hysterical distempers, etc.* Cheyne blamed this apparently new phenomenon squarely on England itself, citing:

> The moisture of our air, the variableness of our weather, the rankness and fertility of our soil, the richness and heaviness of our food, the wealth and abundance of the inhabitants, the inactivity and sedentary occupations of the better sort (among whom this Evil mostly rages) and the Humour of living in great, populous and consequently unhealthy Towns, which have brought forth a class and set of distempers, with atrocious and frightful symptoms, scarce known to our Ancestors, and never rising to such fatal heights, nor afflicting such numbers in any other known nation. These nervous Disorders being computed to make almost one third of the complaints of the people of condition in England.

Feel free to reinterpret the data. Anxiety next appeared during the French Revolution, and in the subsequent two hundred years was rediscovered and labeled as, variously: soldier's heart, cardiac neurosis, nervous exhaustion, neurocirculatory asthenia, neurasthenia, hysteria, and effort syndrome. Soldiers seem to have been prime candidates for such diagnoses, perhaps because they were expected to be stout and brave: when they weren't, they must be ill. Women, on the other hand, could faint and hyperventilate and shriek at will, and no one would think there was anything wrong, just the typical feminine delicacy. Post-traumatic stress disorder was almost certainly one of the earliest variants of anxiety to be noticed—but in soldiers, not in raped and beaten women, whose traumas went unrecognized.

Nobody who was merely anxious or depressed (or however they might have constructed their experience) would go near the asylums—which were the only secular venues for treatment of psychological pain—because of the stigma. Interestingly, the alienists themselves inadvertently created this stigma, by inventing a nonsensical but hugely influential theory called "degeneration." In 1857, the French doctor Benedict-Augustin Morel announced to the world that madness was passed from one generation to the next, and that it grew steadily worse. If a grandfather were alcoholic, then his son would be, let us say, a "cretin," and the grandson would be an alcoholic cretin with delusions of grandeur. Once an insufficiency of character was discovered in a family, the genetic line would steadily erode in character until that family was doomed.

Amazingly, this theory spread all over Europe and North America as if it were plausible. One result—not including that really big result that had to do with justifying the holocaust—was that families began concealing their mentally ill relatives, in order to protect their children's marriage prospects. Thus, the tradition of the mad aunt in the attic was born. Ironically, the excitedly imagined theory of degeneration plunged the care of the acutely mentally ill back into the disturbing days prior to asylums, when families were entirely responsible for their insane kin and kept them chained to barn walls, to fences, or—in rural Ireland—in pits. (The English disowned demented relatives and drove them away, condemning them to wandering vagrancy, whence comes the image of the village idiot.)

Another result of the wariness people felt about the asylums, once the theory of degeneration was in wide circulation, was that the locus of minor mental illness shifted, by popular necessity, from the mind to the nerves. If you could be said to have a "nervous illness," you could confidently explain that your condition was physical, and completely distinct from a "mental illness"; therefore it wouldn't lead to familial degeneration. It was more like getting the flu. Once this idea was floated by a handful of influential neurologists, people began speaking openly again about relatives who suffered from melancholy or panic or another variant of emotional distress, for it could all be safely subsumed under the title of "nerves."

What suffering from nerves actually meant depended upon the self-appointed expert you consulted. In the United States, the neurologist George Beard called the condition "neurasthenia," and further characterized it as a culture-bound trait that he dubbed "American nervousness." Beard felt that it had to do with unique American pressures to succeed, besetting those "in the higher walks of business life, who are in deadly earnest in the race for place and power." Women were particularly vulnerable to neurasthenia, because they weren't used to challenging their brains and swiftly grew exhausted. As the historian Elaine Showalter notes, "an elaborate system of cures, including nerve tonics, galvanic belts, electric faradization, health spas, and retreats catered to the prosperous neurasthenic seeking help for his (or her) sexual problems or nervous exhaustion."

Meanwhile in Europe, Jean-Martin Charcot, chief physician at the Salpetriere hospice in Paris, was busy homing in on the condition of "hysteria." Unlike neurasthenia, which was entirely modern, the term hysteria had been around since Aristotle and had tended to refer to a physical condition associated with the womb, but in a magnificently vague manner, as in "the wandering womb," so that women availed themselves of sips of "hysteric water" to treat everything from menstrual cramps to rage.

Charcot recast hysteria as an affliction that specifically involved changes in nerve tissue. He devised the "iron laws of hysteria" as a diagnostic guide for physicians confronted with ailments ranging from headache to paralysis, and then trotted out women—at his weekly Paris lectures—who had fled to his hospital as victims of brutality and rape, to act as his unwitting cases in point. Some of these women even gained celebrity, as if they were hapless guests on the *Jerry Springer Show*. These iron laws of hysteria were as manifestly ridiculous as the theory of degeneration, but the idea of hysteria (as a catchphrase or signifier for what we now call anxiety disorders) took flight in Europe through Charcot's showmanship. Not only did the diagnosis fend off the declarative doom of degeneration, but it also played into the Victorian ideal of female frailty. Hysteria's symptoms, such as dizziness, upset stomach, and headache, enabled women who were anxious, depressed, or who just didn't feel like going out with a boring suitor on a given evening, to suffer from attacks and collapse on their settees.

Eventually, this conflation of the word hysteria with weak femininity caused the term to be tossed out, and the proverbial baby went out with the bathwater. Recently, neuropsychiatrists have been able to confirm through brain imaging that such fascinating phenomena as hysterical paralysis actually do exist. Somatic symptoms are very real; the mind has a powerful effect on the body. But in the nineteenth century, the contributions of mind, body, soul, culture, and gender to the experience of anxiety were poorly understood and often very prejudicially assumed. (I can't say with any confidence that the twentieth century improved on this mix, as my own experience will attest, but there have certainly been some valuable insights gleaned.)

By the middle of the nineteenth century, the idea of biologically driven bad moods was proving keenly attractive to medical entrepreneurs. With hysteria, neurasthenia, and melancholy construed as physical illnesses, physical treatments could be dreamed up and sold to the populace. The measurable standard of success with medicine was much higher with the major mental illnesses: if someone is psychotic, and you feed them a dandelion, and they're still psychotic, you know. If they are merely depressed, and you spray them with a hose, they may cheer up, and it may have nothing whatever to do with your hose, but who knows? Water cures at health spas exploded in popularity in Victorian England. The pseudoscientific language surrounding these cures was wonderfully detailed. What spa you went to depended upon what that spa's particular spring water was "indicated" for—with one water deemed best for melancholy, while another cured hysteria. Darwin regularly tried to wrest free of hypochondria by getting sprayed while he stood dutifully naked at a spa in Malvern. Jane Welsh Carlyle, the wife of Thomas Carlyle, wrote wryly to her husband from that same resort: "Admired the fine air and country; found by degrees water, taken as a medicine, to be the most destructive drug I had ever tried—and thus paid my tax to contemporary stupor, and had done with water cure."

Climate came into play for a while in the formulation of correct destinations for treatment; it was argued that the best spas for treating neurotic patients were in the hot and humid Italian Riviera, whereas melancholics were better served by the crisp, alpine air of Switzerland. (The great T. S. Eliot went to recover from his depression on the shores of Lake Geneva.) At some point, diet entered the regimen as well, and neurotic patients opted for a specially formulated blend of enforced isolation with milk feeding that had been popularized by the bestselling American book *Fat and Blood* by physician Silas Mitchell. As Shorter notes, these "supposed indications were nothing short of a triumph of public relations." *Plus ça change.*

The ultimate effect of the newfangled treatments for the physical problem of nerves was to bring minor mental illness into everyday conversation. Americans, in particular, got wholly swept up in the idea of "healthy mindedness." As the Harvard psychologist William James observed at the turn of that century, "The mind-cure principles are beginning so to pervade the air that one catches their spirit at second-hand. One hears of the 'Gospel of Relaxation' and the 'Don't Worry Movement,' of people who repeat to themselves 'Youth! Health! Vigour!' when dressing in the morning, as their motto for the day."

In this exciting new endeavor of engaging in mental hygiene, another discovery was made. The neurologists who were treating nervous conditions through spa and diet and the like began to notice that their patients were benefiting as much from the doctor-patient relationship *itself* as from the treatment. Being able to confide to a listener without fear of opprobrium— that seemed to be working an unexpected kind of magic. Perhaps what people really wanted was to talk, and to be heard—not as sinners in the confessional, but as individuals. Maybe they wanted their experience acknowledged—to have someone bear witness, say "Yes, indeed, your life is on fire." Just as this realization was dawning, along came a neurologist named Sigmund Freud, who had studied hysterics with

Charcot in Paris and returned to establish a patient base in Vienna that included a large number of very bright young Jewish women, to whom nobody had ever listened. Whether or not these women—articulate, frustrated and undervalued—specifically benefited from being held up as case studies of hysterics with penis envy has become a matter of bitter dispute. But it was through their encounters with the ambitious and curious neurologist that office-based talk therapy as a medical rather than spiritual approach to emotional turmoil arrived on the scene.

If the German alienist Emil Kraepelin took charge of naming and classifying the major mental illnesses, it was Freud who stamped his foot and cried out for semantic order amongst the minor ones. In place of hysteria, neurasthenia, and so on, Freud established the term "anxiety neurosis," which remained the dominant diagnosis for what I found myself suffering in Chicago some eighty years later. The 1968 *Diagnostic and Statistical Manual of Mental Disorders* (DSM) described anxiety neurosis as "characterized by anxious over-concern extending to panic, and frequently associated with somatic symptoms."

Had I presented, with these symptoms, to an American psychiatrist between 1945 and 1975, I would very likely have been asked about my relationship with my mother, and about my subconscious sexual drives. Had I presented after 1963, I might have been offered the benzodiazapine Valium, as an adjunct to conversation. Had I been in California in the late 1970s, I might have been asked to roar like a lion or write down my dreams or rebirth myself through a tunnel of blankets. Therapies and medicines were being continuously invented and experimentally applied. One's treatment was essentially a matter of happenstance—to whom one was sent on the advice of a friend of a friend. As it happened, I was referred to a psychiatrist at a teaching hospital who believed that I was the sum of my brain cells and that nothing would help but a drug.

The lithium made my hands tremble; it gave me such a dry mouth that I felt like I'd been force-fed saltines. I tossed it after three weeks. In the meantime, the passage of unharried days in the nonjudgmental and serene environment of my sister's home appeared to have gradually restored my equilibrium. Light began returning to the world, and I was surprised by the sensation. "Like her remembrance of awakened birds, or her desire for June and evening," wrote Wallace Stevens in his poem "Sunday Morning." The reward of illness is its tenderheartedness; I was still deeply sensitive in the aftermath, but sensitive to wonder, now, instead of danger. I even took a trip back to Chicago in early summer to photograph parts of the ghetto known then as Cabrini-Green. I felt strengthened, creative, possessed of new ardor. By autumn, I was eager and excited to go down to New York and attend Columbia's Graduate School of Journalism, to which I'd applied from Dundas. I could take on the world now, it seemed. And more than that, I felt obliged to, for it shamed me that I'd failed in Chicago for such a seemingly trivial reason as thwarted love. But there was a problem—one that I wouldn't understand for several more years. What is it that they say about addiction? There is a difference between recovery and sobriety? Well indeed, where the health of one's mind is concerned, there is a difference between recovery and wisdom.

I hadn't gained any insight into what it was, in the collision between my particular psyche and my specific culture, that had sickened me. What I knew, what my story revealed to me then, at the age of twenty-three at the end of the 1980s, was that I had recovered from heartbreak—hurrah! Just as friends had urged and doctors had ordered! I was game to follow my wide-eyed curiosity into new adventures. Precisely *why* it was that my curiosity, as soon as I arrived in New York, would tend toward charming serial killers and charismatic mobsters didn't occur to me. Why would it have, when the entire culture was similarly in thrall? Scarcely did I imagine, at the time, that I myself was about to become the protagonist in a cautionary tale.

4

A Life of Crime

We are like a lot of wild spiders crying together, but without tears.

—ROBERT LOWELL

THE AUTUMN that I arrived in New York, crime was very much the rage in conversation. It had the air of nineteenth-century parlor gossip—a frisson of menace without, in fact, a real sense of threat. There hadn't yet been school shootings on the scale we now contend with, and there certainly wasn't any apprehension about terrorists, domestic or foreign. Crack-driven crime was unsettling, as was gang violence. But for the most part, people engaged in a kind of excited dinner party chatter about celebrity criminals—the mafiosos and the serial killers. That fall, Ted Bundy was approaching his date with retribution in Florida, which was the talk of my criminal justice reporting class. Bundy was offering to confess to more savagery, and he wanted to talk about pornography, how and why it was to blame for the way he had murdered more than thirty women in secret, while otherwise studying law.

Everyone in the class knew about Bundy. He was as much a household name then as a Brad Pitt is now. The first wave of serial killer accounts had just washed across the bookstore shelves, making true crime writers like Ann Rule as famous as such novelists as Danielle Steel. The many instant converts (mostly women) to the spare, plodding paperbacks being published about Bundy and his ilk were fervently attracted to the subject. "His courage bowls you over. His brutality makes you shudder," Diderot once wrote, setting the murderer apart from the crooked politician or humdrum thief. The serial killer was portrayed as darkly romantic, mysterious, savage; he embodied something that women were fascinated by—a sense of deceptive presence.

It wasn't casual fascination, although it appeared to be. Most of the killers were described as seductive; they often volunteered and did good works. They could have been our lovers. *They could have been our lovers*—that was the point of the intense, if inarticulate, interest. Because, of course, we needed to know, however unconsciously: what are the markers that point to a good man, now that men can lie beside us and use us and leave us and roll their eyes in disbelief at such antiquated notions as honor? Fair enough, no need for honor. But *what* then? What are the signifiers of trustworthy conduct?

So we read about men like Bundy in books such as Ann Rule's *The Stranger Beside Me*, evincing a distant armchair interest in the subject, and slowly our fear of criminality began to creep upward like a chill along the spine. There were a number of contributors, of course, to our mounting sense of unease: media headlines, movies, emerging cop shows, and figures in law enforcement trying to fortify their budgets and their reputations. All these factors slowly swirled together into hysteria. By the early nineties, crime was the top American concern in Gallup polls for the first time in fifty years. This notwithstanding the fact that most people continued to perish from strokes, or the flu, or bad driving. We were paying what the psychologists of anxiety call "selective attention to threat." Between 1993 and 1994, during which time the serial killer Jeffrey Dahmer was arrested in Milwaukee, the number of Americans who saw violent crime as the nation's number-one problem quadrupled. In *one year*.

Later, I would have a long, late-night conversation with Dahmer's mother, an incredibly smart woman who was a social worker in California and whose life focus had become her phone calls to her son in prison, trying to understand why he'd done what he'd done. "Were you afraid?" she had asked him. "All the time," he'd admitted, "I was so afraid of what I was doing, Mom." But that complexity was lost before it was found. Dahmer was instantly iconographic. His mother told me about renting a movie one night, and the clerk telling her a "Dahmer joke."

While I was at Columbia, I was one of the female true crime afficionados, and I decided to focus my reporting on crime, because, as I saw it at the time, in New York the cops and robbers were so extremely vivid that other subjects paled by comparison. Crime, after all, was an ingredient in Manhattan's glamour at the time. The city seemed proud to be irascible and tough, playing home to self-consciously hard-boiled journalists like Jimmy Breslin, clever prosecutors like Rudolph Giuliani, and cool criminals from both the white-collar and mafia milieus. The city was incorrigibly macho, and the energy and style with which it corrupted one's sense of glamour was thrilling.

One big event during that time was the racketeering trial of John Gotti, boss of the Gambino crime family, which I covered with huge excitement, as if I'd been given tickets to the Super Bowl or an invitation to the Oscars. Gotti's associates were easy to spot, because nobody else in the room looked like gangsters. The associates swaggered in and out with the *New York Post* jammed into the crook of their arms, mouthing off about that day's coverage to anyone with a pen, scanning the room for celebrities, and monopolizing the pay phones. A reporter from *New York Newsday* gained close access to them by running a column called "Today's Gotti Garb," which featured the best gangster outfit in court on a given day. On the morning that Gotti's defense attorney, Anthony Cardinale, described the proceedings as "the most important criminal trial in America today," Gotti Garb featured an exotic fuchsia and mandarin tie.

Excitement multiplied a thousandfold when Sammy "The Bull" Gravano took the stand. This was because Gotti's former underboss could confirm the FBI's speculations. He could say, in effect, "Yeah, we're mobsters. We are not zipper salesmen. We bully companies into giving us tons of money, after which they go bankrupt, and then we hijack trucks."

Gotti's defense attorneys seemed to be experiencing a constant impulse to jump up, rush over, and stuff socks in Gravano's mouth.

The media had the opposite reaction. They never, never wanted Gravano to shut up again in his whole life. He made the Godfather movies come to life, and that, I presume, is where the writers were culling their narrative cues; the more Gravano talked, the more the newspapers denounced him for being a traitor—not to the city, which he had turned upside down and shaken until all the change fell out, but to his friend. "Betrayal," one famous columnist penned solemnly in his notebook, underlining the word three times. The next day, I read the columnist's account of how the Dapper Don was "stoic" and "graceful" in the presence of the best friend who'd "shamelessly" turned on him. That is not what I recall. I have a distinct memory of Gotti entertaining himself by plucking his attorney's handkerchief out of his pocket, wrapping it around his head and pretending he was a bandit.

Gotti was no Tony Soprano. He was stupid, brutal, and childish, but that wasn't a narrative of choice for New Yorkers, or for most Americans who went on to find the *The Sopranos* to be riveting and emotionally realistic TV. The actor Anthony Quinn even showed up at the court one day to express his sympathy for the Don's predicament. "I grew up in a tough neighborhood too," he said to the reporters amassed on the courthouse steps. "I know the importance of friendship." Let's be clear. This man, John Gotti, who presented himself officially and for tax purposes as "a zipper salesman," had murdered dozens of human beings. He didn't have panic attacks, like Tony Soprano. He wasn't complicated. He was greedy.

Not everyone felt sentimental about him. Most of the curmudgeons resided in the New York City Police Department, headquartered in a fifteen-story building in lower Manhattan. They hated the sleekly spun theories of the experts and FBI agents whose stars were then ascending in the culture of criminal celebrity. They figured no one had the right to open their mouths until they'd slogged through a garbage dump looking for body parts and then broken the news to a parent. For me, as a young journalism student, these cops were just as captivating as the criminals.

"I have no trouble with schizophrenia," one detective offered, when I went to see him about a case involving an insanity defense. "I understand that people get sick. I got no problem with that. I just wanna know one thing. How come the voices in their heads always say 'kill your mooth-err . . . kill them aaalll . . .' How come they never say 'get a jooobbb . . .'?"

That, obviously, is the flair that makes such men the template for Hollywood films and TV series, but at the time I was fascinated by the insanity defense. It seemed to me that the boundaries were untraceable, no matter what the legal plea, that no act could be deemed strictly sane or insane. What was sane about Bundy bursting into a sorority house in Tallahassee, Florida, with a wooden board in one hand, maniacally darting from room to room and clubbing every woman he found as if on a seal hunt? What unfamiliar guise of sanity had the Florida courts insisted upon for that? Maybe I was trying to follow the thread of my own life in this walkabout I took through our criminal culture. In retrospect, I can't say that it was purposive, this unconscious quest for boundaries and absolutes, for visible markers, only that it grew extraordinarily dark.

One winter after journalism school, in my customary flux between freelance gigs, I met a man at an East Village party who looked like Paul Simon with beadier eyes. He had tired of his family cosmetics business and wanted to become a TV producer. Impulsively, he offered me a job on a series he aimed to create called *Confessions of Crime*. The show, he explained, would feature videotaped statements made by killers, gathered from boxes of trial evidence stashed away in state courthouses. The practice of videotaping suspects' statements was new then. He had hit upon a gimmick that could get him into the fledgling realm of infotainment. I seemed to know stuff about criminal psychology. That could help him, he figured.

A month later, he hired two alarmingly aggressive journos from the tabloid show *Hard Copy* to package the video into half-hour stories. I was the field producer, the one who would find the cases and talk to the people whose worlds had ended, and persuade them that it was somehow in their interest to have private loss and sorrow molded into quick jolts of entertainment on TV. In long, tender telephone conversations with murderers, I let them know I understood, and I did begin to understand a little. How the son reared up and destroyed the hectoring, demeaning father; how the mother finally just needed to punish, punish, punish the child who'd been indifferent to her—had "conduct disorder"—had been out of control for so long; how the wife could no longer bear the apprehension of attack from a battering husband. How the slow accumulation of insults erodes one's composure until there's nothing left but the grabbed-up knife and the "Fuck you, FUCK YOU!" in a vibrant black rage.

Perhaps there would be healing through service to others, I'd tell them. "If we could just let other parents know the dangers of keeping guns in the house . . ." "People need to understand child abuse, what it does . . ." Behind me in our renovated loft office on lower Broadway, I'd hear the *Hard Copy* producers slamming down the phone after their own calls, yelping "Got 'em! Yeah!" like they were shooting skeet.

The show's executive producer was a bored, expatriate Oxford Brit who drank too much. One night, he took me out for Chardonnay and lamented the banality of his show. "You cannot say 'Hard Copy' and 'Bosnia' in the same sentence without experiencing a midlife crisis," he muttered, swiping my last cigarette. "It's an impossibility."

But he knew as well as anyone that it was impossible for people to follow the unfolding events in Bosnia, and that everyone yearned to discuss something, together, collectively.

So, "bang, bang, you're dead." The import was obvious. Everyone could play. Vote for or against O. J. Simpson, Lorena Bobbitt, Rodney King. We were using violence to construct something else, a collective understanding; building a public discourse from the dead.

We did not illuminate violence on *Confessions of Crime.* Our phone conversations were bait, a lure to the camera. Once the killers were up on the screen, the script denounced them as "monstrous" and "evil," which maybe would have meant something, if we'd meant it, but we didn't know what violence meant at all. In the end, I came upon death casually, in an inappropriately short dress, which I'd pulled on frantically after waking late one morning to find the impatient, sighing producers waiting outside my SoHo walk-up in their limo. I was in the business of making violence visual, yet violence had never been visible to me. Now I needed to see some crime scene photos for a dramatic reenactment on our show. In the Nassau County Police Department, the good-humored, polyester-suited detectives greeted us with vending machine coffee and jokes. They had time to kill, I suppose. Either that, or TV was a god to whom they could not resist being supplicant. We were there about a boy who'd shot his parents with a high-powered rifle when they opposed his choice of girlfriend.

I sat down with my coffee at a borrowed desk and began to sift through the snaps. I found the boy's mother in her immaculate kitchen, flat on her back on the floor. Her striped cotton skirt had flown up above her plump waist to reveal her fully—her baggy blue panties, her clammy white thighs. This was none of my business. Her head, which had taken the bullet and exploded, lay cradled on a loaf of bloody Wonder Bread. The gunshot had blown her tongue clear out of her mouth. I found it in another picture in the pile, sitting atop her white microwave oven. What this was, I thought, was ignominy. Abandonment. Erasure.

These were the kinds of pictures that NBC ought to have aired last year, instead of the self-aggrandizing hero shots provided to them by the stone-eyed boy who gunned down thirty-two people at Virginia Tech. To see not the artifice of death, but its chaotic and annihilating truth; maybe that would end such sickening quests for infamy.

One Christmas, I went to visit my sister in Dundas, the one who'd helped me to recover from my first breakdown. Her husband was ferrying me past the town square in his mini-van, having fetched me from the bus, and a crowd had gathered there, milling around a platform. "Are they organizing a search for a missing child?" I asked. My brother-in-law gave me a long, studious look of bemusement. "No," he said. "They're singing Christmas carols, Patricia."

I had been a crime reporter for some years by this time, tunneling into the minds of vile men, gazing at the faces of strangled boys and mutilated women, sitting for hours in a car in the pouring rain while the father of a dead child sobbed, taking notes. I'd like to say that I was taunting myself on purpose, testing my courage, but it wasn't like that. It was an act of empathy that I was good at, this was the world I felt I knew. After the journalist Tim Cahill finished writing his book about John Wayne Gacy, he locked his office door and walked away, intending to return that afternoon. He could not walk back through it for a year. I do remember reading that somewhere, and finding it interesting and missing the point.

When the murderer made his literary debut in the nineteenth century, via Poe, Dostoyevsky and Stendhal, he was a secular adaptation of Satan, still connected to the great moral quandaries, to the cautionary tale. By my time, the vocabulary was thinly scientific. Killers were case studies. One examined them without, in fact, a discernible sense of moral separateness. In studies of exposure to trauma, one occasionally finds the question posed as to who survives the trauma most intact, and why. Of psychologically healthy Vietnam vets, the authors of one study note, "These men had consciously focused on preserving their calm, their judgment, their connection with others, their moral values and their sense of meaning."

Looking back over my letters and journals, I trace the growth of a certain deformity in my perception. A tendency to witness the behavior of lovers and friends as menacing. A dark imagining of desire as predation, my seducers as psychopaths, or myself as the one who was dangerous. I dreamt that I was a poisoner's accomplice, working furtively and senselessly, perspiration pricking my neck.

My family doctor began taking a look at my mental health

for the first time. How much coffee? Any drugs? Family history of anxiety? Symptoms, past symptoms? Did any doctors treat me? I got her involved inadvertently, through seeking out a prescription for Xanax to quell my sudden fear of flying. I didn't see that fear as connected to anything else. Such as fear of loving, fear of the dark, fear of wind, a pervading sense of doom. It had been eight years since my breakdown in Chicago. I had moved back to Toronto. More men had sampled and left me. I'd gone to see a psychic to ask when this would end, when love would come, and she told me I was allergic to cheese.

Out of this hall of mirrors, in the summer of 1995, came a pair of murderers named Paul Bernardo and Karla Homolka. I hate even writing their names. Good-looking kids from good families, good marks in college, good manners, watched *The Simpsons*, loved thrillers, infatuated with themselves, went up the river and hooked up with Kurtz. They were not all that different from the people I went to school with except that they recorded rapes on their camcorder alongside their wedding ceremony and a Disney vacation. (The three adolescents they murdered off lens, offering the court opposite, self-exonerating scenarios for what happened.)

We are accustomed to this now, this incessant self-recording, every life a pitch for brief celebrity on YouTube. We were destined to encounter the home videos of psychopaths, but we were wholly unprepared. Days and days of intolerable evidence in a Toronto courtroom as the heat hit one hundred degrees on the sidewalk outside. We heard young women being sexually assaulted as if we were there, listening behind a locked door. Sixty people hunched over with their eyes on the floor. "Pleeeeeeeeeese," the victim wails, it's so loud, winding upward into a sustained shriek. I walked out of the courtroom after that wail, yelling bitterly at a fellow re-porter, striding fast toward the doors. I hit the street and zig-zagged aimlessly, I could not think and I finally gave up, sinking to my knees on a patch of grass in a traffic circle. The traffic rumbled around me, the light began to slant, and after a while—a few absently smoked cigarettes—I remembered where I belonged, what my geography was, where I was meant to be in the world. I hailed a cab to a friend's.

In the early twilight, I sat with my friend's child in the garden, watching her twirl about smiling with her love-worn security blanket, tossing it up into the lilac tree, then shaking it free, so that it fluttered down to cover her, I thought how the murder victim Leslie Mahaffy's mother must once have watched her tiny child, spinning and wheeling, and suddenly Natalie's blanket became the T-shirt tied around Mahaffy's eyes. All evening, objects of delight transformed themselves into instruments of horror. I felt as though I were inflicting that on Natalie somehow. Bringing depravity with me like a rank scent into the garden, lurking beneath the perfume of the lilac, something rotten.

In the autumn of Bernardo's imprisonment, I took a studio apartment in New York's West Village to complete some re-porting for a book on violent women. The specter of horror was everywhere, taking its stylish turn through the culture, spooking me as I came around corners. I went to see *Seven* at the suggestion of a friend. The film's savagery was thought to be clever: How often do you see a victim forced to eat until his stomach explodes? Or a man made to bleed to death by cutting a pound of his own flesh? Dazzling innovations for a crowd grown bored by gunfire. I exited the cinema in a state of speechless jitters.

I wandered into the Guggenheim one day and came across an exhibit of still lifes with Mexican corpses and fruit. The photographer Joel Peter Witkin had purchased bodies from coroners, dragged them to his studio and dressed them in hoop skirts. Patrons were gazing appraisingly at severed feet on platters surrounded by pears. I ran into someone at a party who knew Bret Easton Ellis, author of *American Psycho*, a novel much loved by Paul Bernardo. Ellis had apparently read up avidly on Bernardo's trial. In Toronto the parents of Bernardo's victims began fighting passionately to have the videotapes destroyed as child pornography. They weren't just courtroom evidence, the parents argued, because the distinction between justice and entertainment could no longer be trusted to hold.

What is the definition of a crime? What should the criminal confess to? To the breaking of a law, or to something else, a criminal indifference, to the breaking of a heart? Whose culpability was I contemplating now? I encountered a mother that autumn whose child had died at her hands. She was to be a case study for my book. An intelligent, middle-class Long Island high school student whose confession had been taped. The Suffolk County DA's office made me a copy, which I watched in my flat. This girl was wary of her interrogator, alarmed by his interest in her teenaged affairs. She told him, because he asked, that she gave birth to a son. And stuffed her son into a garbage bag—because that was where a mess belonged—and drove around for the day paying visits to pals, announcing to those who knew she'd been pregnant that she'd had a miscarriage.

She asked me in a letter not to use her story in my book. "Go to hell," I thought, and succumbed to a harrowing insomnia. I turned my traumatized attention to my body. I was flesh bereft of spirit, like Witkin's chopped-up props, a friable self, grotesque. I couldn't imagine myself being healthy enough to have children and grew convinced I had grown infertile. I got an AIDS test. I had my moles checked. I grew suspicious of pains in my back. If I was nauseous, I worried about cancer and started reading up obsessively on symptoms. I lay in bed whenever I could, trying to shut up the clamor of terror with sleep.

Someone suggested Christmas in the country. I gathered together dear friends and a new boyfriend, and ventured into the hills of Quebec to a winterized cabin. The snow was a blanket of white velvet. The maple trees sparkled with ice. The woodstove in the cabin made our faces glow. But my panic was fierce and more piercing than cold, and I kept it to myself. I took a solitary morning walk along the road and heard the sound of footsteps crunching. They came from behind me, crunch, crunch. There was only that sound, not even distant traffic, not wind. A slowing of the steps, a hesitancy, another crunch. My mind cartwheeled through the options. If I screamed, would my friends hear? Should I talk my way out of the encounter? I knew from my reporting that rape victims can luck out either way. But it's either way. It depends on the rapist.

Buzzing with adrenaline, bracing, I stopped and turned. I saw a little girl, eight or ten, stomping balls of ice beneath her boots. I stood there for so long after she passed that the shadows shifted. I was silenced by amazement. Not at my fear, but at the girl. It was just a fact that I could not quite get through my head. That she could walk alone through the woods; that she was not afraid.

I got into my small used Mazda and tried to drive to a nearby town for groceries, but the temperature outside had dropped steeply. I realized, with an awful, shocked dread, that if I turned the key in the ignition the car would explode. "Oh God," I whispered, and fetched my friends, cutting in on their round of poker, speaking sharply, "This is not a joke!" Gamely, they swept snow from their station wagon and followed behind as I inched my way toward the mechanic up the road, panting, barely able to swallow, my eyes as round as the eyes of a woman I once saw in a Polaroid photo, snapped by her killer in the beat before oblivion.

I cannot say that I wanted this madness to end, because a part of the madness was my inability to want without apprehension, to envisage a life without calamity, to make a simple wish. "To cease wishing is to be dead," Rollo May once ventured, "or at least to inhabit the land of the dead, for without faith, we cannot want anymore, we cannot wish." May quoted Eliot: "What shall I do now? What shall I do? Pressing lidless eyes and waiting for a knock upon the door."

"Can I wish this much?" I asked one night, six years after graduating from journalism school, having sat in arid terror in the bathtub for an hour: to rise from the tepid water and walk into the living room and listen to music that moves me? I needed to wish this much, and I knew it. I got up on dull legs and pulled out the CD *Grace* by an emerging new singer, Jeff Buckley. His voice was peculiarly beautiful, suffused with a sorrow that is rarely articulated in my vernacular, for my age. He sang of attending a funeral. "I wish they hadn't died," I said aloud to my empty apartment, trying to think of things to wish. It was an odd, uncertain sentiment that grew, as when a dry bit of ritual unexpectedly swells with meaning. Curled into my hand-me-down futon I felt the tension in me snap, and grief broke through. I wept for the girls who had wailed for my help, the boy left strangled beneath a tree, the mother hurled onto the kitchen floor, my own lost child, for the obscenity, for the absence of consecration. I let the tears slide blindly through my hands, I couldn't stop, I did not want to, I wept for hours.

Near the house I bought a few years later with my husband, who is a kind, perceptive man, only wicked in his wit, there is a lovely little park. It has a farm—an actual working farm that sells eggs on Tuesday afternoons. The farm has two horses, six pigs, and three cows. The people who work there wear red T-shirts.

"I want to work on a farm," I told Ambrose one afternoon. I had left crime reporting behind, switched to more light-hearted writing. I was attracted to a world that felt rooted and placid.

"That's fine," Ambrose said, "but you'd have to do chores."

"Oh, that's true," I laughed. "Never mind." I hadn't been very domestic in the time that he'd known me. Certain things, though, I was having to learn how to do. I walked across the grass with baby Clara on my hip. My love is my weight, wrote Saint Augustine. Because of it, I move.

5

Fear's Geography

In a sense, every human construction, whether mental or material, is a component in a landscape of fear because it exists to contain chaos. Thus children's fairy tales as well as adults' legends, cosmological myths and indeed philosophical systems are shelters built by the mind in which human beings can rest, at least temporarily, from the siege of inchoate experience and of doubt.

—YI-FU TUAN, *LANDSCAPES OF FEAR*

IT IS SAINT Patrick's Day, and my godmother and I are motoring past jacaranda trees in ebullient lavender bloom as we head from the Mexican city of Cuernavaca—literally "cow's horn," although it's more romantically known as the city of eternal spring—to the pueblo of Tepoztlán, on the high plateau of central Mexico. This area is where the author Malcolm Lowry wrote his wonderfully depressing novel *Under the Volcano*, about a diplomat intent upon killing himself through drink. It is also where I came to recover from sitting through murder trials, and where Ambrose and I brought our little family to live in 2003.

Margaret, who is my godmother, has been living in Mexico for decades. She was great friends with my mother when the two were young wives in Mexico City in the early 1960s. They would head off for girls' weekends every now and then, and dine in far-flung restaurants off the tourist track, where the bathroom toilet paper once famously consisted of spoiled ballots. Much laughter and curiosity and visits to markets, before returning to their respective baby boom broods. When I was born—*Señora, una niña!*—Margaret became my *madrina*. Ever since, she has been the thread connecting me to the country of my birth.

More than once, in the weeks and months that I've spent all over Mexico, including at Margaret's home in Cuernavaca, I have wondered if growing up here, rather than in Canada, would somehow have shaped my temperament differently. Perhaps a life lived in this landscape would have lightened my spirit, or at least foreshortened my stretches of anguish. Mexico has a much lower rate of clinically significant anxiety, according to the World Health Organization's 2002 World Mental Health Survey Initiative. While the levels of specific phobia are roughly similar, a person is four times more likely to suffer from generalized anxiety disorder in the United States than in Mexico, and about three times more likely in Canada. In other words, while we all scream at spiders, it is the upper two affluent nations of North America that are more prone to dread, and to panic. Moreover, the *intensity* of anxiety gets more severe as you head north. When Mexicans are beset by what they (and other Latin Americans) call *ataques de nervios*, they recover their composure twice as quickly. Their stresses are great: poverty, domestic violence, crime in the border cities and in the urban centers. But there simply isn't a great deal of existential gnawing on the furniture. The difference is really brought home by the fact that when Mexicans migrate to Texas, California, and Arizona, their rates of anxiety, depression, and substance abuse suddenly soar. (When in Rome . . .)

Margaret and I consider this question as we lunch at the Tepoztlán *mercado*, trading a handful of pesos at a vendor's stall for blue corn tortillas grilled with mild cheese, zucchini flowers, and corn fungus. "In Canada, the farmers call it corn *smut*, and toss out the crop," Margaret notes, "but here it's a delicacy." I wash my food down with a bottle of mango-flavored Boing and ponder the decapitated goats' heads lined up neatly one stall over, a mute little audience staring dully at the scenery of ripe avocados, deeply red tomatoes, freshly roasted pumpkin seeds, sleek black chiles, and plump, good-humored vendors in sleeveless T-shirts presiding over their sales with easy grace and civility.

"In Mexico," Margaret muses, "it is said that people work in order to have holidays." By this, she means that they do not work for material gain or for personal status, so much as for the freedom to be with their families and friends. Imagine that, I think to myself, having just read an article in the *Toronto Globe and Mail* warning that "Family life interference at work can lead to a stalled career." In Toronto it is best not to have families. In Mexico it is best not to have careers.

We leave the market stalls and wend our way past a group of taxi drivers, who are playing penny poker on the hood of one of their rusted-out VW Bugs. "It's also *how* they spend their free time," Margaret adds, watching the crowd. "They are not alone, isolated in their houses. They go down to the zocalo, and there's always music and balloons, and the parents dress their children nicely."

Incongruously, there is an Irish pub in Tepoztlán, and so the town's people, being Catholic and fond of saints' days, as well as of any opportunity for a fiesta, are out in full swing this Saint Patrick's Day. By Monday, they will be festive all over again for Benito Juarez Day, and shortly after that come the two glorious weeks of Semana Santa, culminating in the festivities of Easter. When we lived here, the effervescent ruckus of mariachi bands and roosters and church bells and incendiary firecrackers took some getting used to. In particular, the sharp report of those infernal crackers, echoing off the volcanic cliff walls, made me jump out of my skin and poke myself in the eye with my mascara wand. Nevertheless, after a while I came to realize that the clangs and bangs and cock-a-doodle-doos were creating an entirely different ambience than the tense sonic atmosphere in the cities that I'd lived in for most of my life—Toronto, Chicago, New York. Instead of the pervasive conveyance of angry alarm presented by police sirens, honking cars, pedestrian vitriol, rude cell conversations, manipulative sales pitches, and aggressive and derisive raps from passing cars, what one hears in Mexico is affirming. Mexico is calling: "Come sing with us, come pray with us, come celebrate." The other worlds I've lived in snarl: "Get out of my way."

Rollo May once wrote, "Competitive individualism militates against the experience of community, and that lack of community is a centrally important factor in contemporaneous anxiety." Could this be the key difference? A community, in Mexico, is not a gated neighborhood or a Starbucks café. When I lived in Tepoztlán, I had neighbors living in half-built houses in the shrubbery, and stray dogs on my lawn. Life crowded in, rather than jostling by. The barriers—between inside and outside, work and family, self and community, life and death, nature and civilization—had never been built. There was everywhere this sense of being connected—fluidly and immediately—to everything around one. In Mexico, the mindfulness guru Jon Kabat-Zinn's adage that "wherever you go, there you are" is not a stress-reduction technique. It is a taken-for-granted truth.

This sense of borderlessness, and of presence, is echoed in the observations made by the geographer Tuan about what kind of landscapes seem to minimize neurosis and fear. One such realm belongs to the Mbuti Pygmies of the central African rain forest. "Unlike most other peoples, the Pygmies live not so much in sacred space, a bounded area or volume, as in an all-encompassing medium," Tuan wrote. Therein lies a major source of their sense of security and freedom from fear. They have no vocabulary for evil. "Without such a concept," Tuan wrote, "there can still be alarm, but the special components of human fear—dread, suspicion, anxiety—are greatly reduced." Yet, why do they lack this concept? In the temperate and fruitful rain forest, their needs are met; they have no need to set themselves apart from their environment, and thus no need to develop a concept of Other.

The historian Paul Newman speculates in A *History of Terror* that the practice of agriculture brought about a new element of fear in human life, because as farmers went about controlling the flora and fauna, they started working at cross-purposes with it, and thus the division of "man" and "beast" began. The forests were no longer a dwelling place; they were a menace. Vermin were no longer food, but threats to crops. It's an interesting speculation. If you look at the great paintings in the Chauvet Cave in southern France, dating back thirty thousand years, you notice that the artists depicted Ice Age animals with a confident blend of realism and reverence, rather than fear. There is no sense of Other.

Tuan made a second observation about the Mbuti that strikes a chord. "Acute awareness of time is a cause of tension and distress in contemporary Western society," he wrote. "Westerners are raised with the burden and challenge of a personal goal, which rests on the idea of time as an arrow pointing toward the successive deadlines of the future. In contrast, the Mbuti have a very weakly developed sense of time. They live in the present. Each day takes care of itself. The past and the future pale into insignificance when compared with the reality of the existential moment." Or, as the Mexicans might say: "*Mañana.*"

On the bus from Cuernavaca to Mexico City—which I

always love, because for twelve dollars you get an assigned seat, an unwatchable Wesley Snipes movie dubbed into Spanish, and free sodas—I find myself sitting next to a South African-trained business psychologist who works in Dallas and has in-laws here. Of my research, he says simply, "The sense of material entitlement so pervasive in the States just doesn't exist here. People feel lucky if they have a roof over their heads." Is this another, paradoxical element in their lessened anxiety? Mexico does have a tiny, quasi-aristocratic class of *ricos,* such as Carlos Slim, the man who owns the phone monopoly Telmex and has managed to surpass Bill Gates as the world's richest individual. This small club of vastly wealthy men and women fortify their garden walls with jagged glass and have developed a fondness for Xanax.

I switch buses at the airport in Mexico City and then head north past the slums, mile upon mile of ashen cinder block squares dotted with flapping laundry in endless treeless rows, like a suburban development in which nothing got built but the garages, hundreds of thousands of people living out their lives in gray cement garages too small, in fact, to house cars. Attenuated half-garages, where paint is a sign of inestimable fortune. To say that these citizens live in Mexico City is a confusing kind of lie, for there is no "city" in these miles of rows, punctuated by junkyards and trash heaps. There's no cinema, or church, or shop, or gas station, or at least none that is visible as distinctive architecture. Yet life carries on in full panoply of religious ritual, fiesta, soccer games, and, according to the artist Edgardo Kerlegand, who grew up in Chiapas and then worked with the residents of these slums, very deep communal support.

The bus climbs gradually higher into the hills that lead to the colonial silver cities of Guanajuato and San Miguel de Allende. My grandmother used to paint in San Miguel. It is an enchanting town filled with spired sixteenth-century churches and cobbled streets. My friend Russell Monk, a photographer, has been renovating a pile of rubble on the outskirts of town for the past couple of years. His neighbor makes one hundred pesos (around eight dollars) a day cleaning a restaurant. Her husband brings in no family income because he's spending what he earns, at the moment, on medications to combat a hex placed on him by his spurned mistress. The hex causes him to shake violently. He is planning to visit a witch to purchase a counterspell. In the meantime, his wife tells Russell, as roughly translated from Spanish: "He's an asshole, but he's *my* asshole."

Russell bought her a toilet and paid for the installation of plumbing; he and his girlfriend take her kids swimming at the hot spring in the hills. Unintentionally, for he sees himself as a gringo with obscene advantages, he has fallen into the communal custom of simply lending a hand. The same thing happened to Ambrose and me in Tepoztlán: you see your neighbors, you see what they need. The boundaries are down, the fences are diminished, the status is immaterial. Everyone shares everyone's business. Of course, as my mother used to say, the downside to that is that "the walls have ears." But what is the alternative in our tony northern cities? When I face financial ruin, which I occasionally nearly do, the stress is all the more acute because of my isolation: nobody knows my business, and they also don't much care.

Russell's girlfriend—also a photographer—is off, just now, acting as a translator for a crew from *National Geographic* magazine, who are preparing a feature on happiness. They're up in Guadalajara exploring why the Mexicans rank so high in the world sample.

"Do you know who ranks the highest?" Russell asks in some amazement, as we leave a restaurant packed with folk celebrating Benito Juarez Day. "The Nigerians!" Russell is Jack Sprat in a borrowed sombrero, tall and lean and in love with Mexico. His voice—warm, rough, and British— invariably reminds me of the comic Eddie Izzard. "How is that possible, have you ever been to Lagos?" His eyes widen in amusement. No, I've never seen the teeming African metropolis with its legions of shanties and mountains of garbage. But I have seen similar data suggesting that Nigerians have one of the lowest rates of anxiety in the world.

Perhaps some light might be shed on this by Dr. Samuel Thielman, director of the Division of Mental Health Services for the U.S. Department of State. Thielman, who has worked in Africa, offered the example of the Nairobi Embassy bombing in 1998, which the Kenyan staff found less traumatic than did the American diplomatic personnel. According to Thielman, the Kenyans chose to interpret the event in terms of the happy luck that they had *survived*. This was their habit of mind. They then framed their survival in terms of an overarching scheme, or "God's plan." Actually, in the case of one employee, it had to do with the lucky number seven, but it's the same idea. "If a patient believes that events occur randomly—outside of a larger story—they will have more anxiety," Thielman told a gathering of his colleagues recently at a symposium on spirituality and mental health.

Certainly, studies consistently reveal that the religiously observant are less prone to severe anxiety and depression. When the question is posed as to why they suffer less, the answer is not that their fear of death is diminished, but that their lives are shaped by a narrative that is larger than themselves. In secular/material cultures, we forgo such narratives in favor of what is actually a more implausible myth: that we can assume total mastery over our fates. This is what my current psychiatrist, who was raised in Mexico City, meant when he told me that the trouble in the affluent North was our "illusion that we have any control."

In today's *New York Times*, I read about a freelance health writer's reaction to her diagnosis of breast cancer. She was consumed with needing to know why. Why did she get cancer—she exercised, she didn't smoke!—how had she lost control? She pored over studies and consulted medical texts until, at length, she came to realize that the answer didn't matter. "I'll never know why I got cancer," she writes. "What I do know is that the sooner I let go of the need to find something or someone to blame, the sooner I'll be able to put cancer behind me and enjoy life, however long or short it may be. Only when I accept the sometimes cruel randomness of fate will I be able to call myself a survivor."

Reading this woman's account put me in mind of a conversation I had on my way to a funeral with a taxi driver in Toronto, an immigrant to Canada from Lagos. He expressed his condolences when I explained where I was going. "It's so awful," I said. "She was too young to die."

"How old?" he asked, glancing into his rearview with sympathy.

"She was only sixty-two," I said.

He laughed in surprise. "That's not too young. Back home, after sixty we say 'there but for the Grace of God.'"

Accepting fate, even acknowledging that there might *be* fate, is so antithetical to the secular West that we scarcely know what to do with the concept. As the historian Alice Bullard has noted, "It is not allowed that we live our lives in resignation to 'fate.' If indeed fate has dealt us an evil or challenging hand we are supposed to fight it and triumph over it." And so we set out, one by one, like cowboys and superheroes, to do battle with the forces of the world.

Historically, that battle was enacted on behalf of the group by its leaders, through highly elaborate rituals that served to offset individual anxiety by providing the illusion that someone was in charge. "Ritual," notes Tuan, "has this in common with scientific procedure or effective practical action: it follows definite and predictable rules. In times of uncertainty, the performance of set gestures can be reassuring in itself." One of the most fascinating examples of this comes from the

Middle Ages, when animals were summoned to court to stand trial, for infringing upon or demolishing the human food supply. Consider, for instance, the court records for "The People Versus Locusts," which took place in southern France in 1338. The bishop's proctor sentenced the locusts after an actual trial by announcing that "the guilt of the accused has been clearly proved by the testimony of worthy witnesses and, as it were by public rumor." Therefore, "we admonish the aforesaid locusts and grasshoppers and other animals by whatsoever name they be called, under pain of malediction and anathema, to depart from the vineyards and fields of this district within six days, from the publication of this sentence and to do no further damage there or elsewhere."

I came across this trial record in a marvelous gem of a book published by an American social historian in 1906, called *The Criminal Prosecution and Capital Punishment of Animals*. It was accepted practice throughout Europe, from about the tenth through the sixteenth centuries, to arrest animals, assign them lawyers, argue their cases incessantly, and then sentence them to a variety of punishments. Pigs went to the gallows, donkeys languished in jail awaiting trial, slugs were excommunicated, moles were sent into exile. In 1519, in Western Tyrol, for example, criminal proceedings were instituted against some field mice and moles "for burrowing and throwing up the earth so that neither grass nor green things could grow." The judge decreed that "in order that said mice be able to show cause for their conduct by pleading their exigencies," they were to be appointed able counsel. A lawyer was hired—it's unclear whether he met with any of his completely unaware clients—and a long list of witnesses then presented for both the prosecution and the defense. After considering all the arguments, the judge ordered banishment, but allowed "a free safe-conduct" or protective escort out of the area, "and additional respite of 14 days is granted to all those which are with young and to such as are yet in their infancy. But on the expiration of this reprieve, each and every one must be gone."

The high-minded judiciousness with which these rodents were tried is echoed in the eminently fair treatment of garden slugs in 1487: "Jean Rohin, Cardinal Bishop of Autun, ordered public processions to be made for three days in every parish, and enjoined upon the slugs to quit the territory within this period under penalty of being accursed." After three warnings, the slugs stubbornly refused to progress more than six inches in any given direction and were regretfully excommunicated.

Sometimes the animals won their cases on appeal. The historian E. P. Evans found an instance where a pig and donkey sentenced to be hanged had their sentences commuted by a higher court to simply being "knocked on the head." Others were not so lucky: in 1394, a pig was hanged at Montaign in France for "having sacrilegiously eaten a consecrated wafer."

While I agree with Evans that these trials reflected the "hair-splitting and syllogistic rubbish which passed for reasoning in the early and middle ages of the Christian era," they do appear to have served a purpose. In situations where communities felt totally powerless over events, these trials provided the illusion that things were under control. Somebody was in charge. Someone—or some creature—was being held to account. It is interesting to contemplate how virtual the medieval world was. Demons were everywhere. Incubi hovered above the beds of nuns. Werewolves and "green men" haunted the forests. Christ was a rock star, inspiring erotic crushes in tweenies, who begged to become his bride. Life was lived as vividly in the realm of imagination—in the spiritual quest, in dreams and fancies and omens—as in the harsh material world. Under the circumstances, it was perfectly plausible that you could excommunicate a slug.

The curious thing is that, while these trials were beautifully absurd, in their absolute fastidiousness and attention to decorum one begins to see the emergence of reason as a new mechanism for keeping anxiety at bay. Reason—so exalted at the moment by überatheists like Richard Dawkins, Sam Harris, and Christopher Hitchens—was at that time reactive, which is to say emotional. It was an emotional response to the failure of spirituality to contain fear in a time of chaos after the retreat of the Roman Empire. Reason—or rationalism, more specifically—evolved out of a need to impose order on a world that was both fraught with danger and haunted by ghosts. As the archaeologist Timothy Taylor has written, "We have forgotten what it is like to be really and truly afraid of malevolent, disembodied spirits, to be haunted by ghosts." *Haunted.* An enormous amount of heartfelt energy was taken up in keeping the spirits appeased. Sitting shiva, for example, which today is a Jewish funerary custom reflecting support for the family and respect for the deceased, was originally a frightening and determined task of guarding a body 24/7 from being reanimated by its soul until it was safely buried.

After the Roman Empire receded from northern Europe, taking with it a sense of orderly governance and pragmatic conduct, the continent fell into a dark age of chaos in every realm, on all levels. The realm of spirit merely added to the fears inherent in this chaos. Newman, for instance, writes about the many world-ending scenarios that sent people off on pilgrimages to the Holy Land. "Despite the inability of the world to end punctually," he notes drily, "these panics persisted down to Luther's age." It is significant, I think, that a patron saint for panic or "les frayeurs" didn't get assigned by the church in Rome until the ninth century. It is also significant that this period marked a transition in Europe between pagan spirits and their well-established customs of observance with the imposition of Christianity. The fear of this "new" God who judged one's conduct spurred charges against others in the community. "They're worse than me!" Our modern need to be reassured that we are not alone was, during the Middle Ages, instead a need to be reassured that someone was worse, more guilty than we were—a more worthy target of spiritual wrath. Anxiety was animated, in this way, by guilt rather than by an absence of meaning.

In part, the clamor to persecute and to demonize—to identify witches and burn heretics—was borne out of this transitional phase. The phenomenon can be laid bare by considering the uses of laughter, then and now. As a humorist writing in the twenty-first century, I see that what appeals to my readers is their ability to connect with what I am saying about small foibles and puzzlements in life: it isn't so much that the foibles and puzzlements are important, as that they usually go unremarked on, and by talking about them, I highlight or uncover commonalities with readers in a way that serves to reassure them that they are not alone. Conversely, in the fourteenth century, humor was aggressive and derogatory and entirely about the need to feel elevated above (spiritually better than) the next person. Thus people offered up their muddied coins for the chance to laugh at lunatics and ridicule the misfits.

Emotions are mutable: they can be shaped by our context, both historic and cultural. The intensity of anxiety felt by modern Westerners may also be connected to the degree to which any of us are encouraged to heed and express our emotions at all. The psychologist Carl Ratner, who does cross-cultural research, has argued that child rearing techniques can influence the propensity to highlight or dwell upon feelings. "Western parents indulge children's emotions and encourage them to pay a great deal of attention" to them, Ratner has said, "while non-Western parents usually do not. The Kipsigis people of Kenya attempt to distract children from emotions. This leads children to de-emphasize personal, internal attributes and become more socially oriented." The psychologist Ruth Chao has noted similar distinctions between styles of American and Chinese socialization. "Forty percent of European-American mothers" in her study "encouraged their children to introspect about, analyze and discuss their feelings, whereas none of the Chinese-American mothers did." It is likely no coincidence that the Chinese also rank very low in the World Mental Health Survey for rates of anxiety. Not only does their socialization discourage them from monitoring their inner psyche—"What does personal anxiety have to do with anything?" as my father might have asked—but it also emphasizes the social connectedness that acts as a buffer *against* anxiety. In other words, their child-rearing techniques guard against the individualistic isolation that evokes such angst in Westerners.

In the seventeenth-century Cathedral of San Francisco, in the colonial city of San Miguel, I walk past a veritable Madame Tussauds wax museum display of gaunt and imploring saints flanking either side of the dark wood pews. They culminate at the altar in a bent-over statue of Christ, bleeding, receiving the soldiers' heavy and humiliating lashes. In Mexico, suffering and death are visually abundant. This is not a culture that feels life's vicissitudes less deeply. What it does do, or so it has always seemed to me, is to acknowledge those sorrows and travails and provide for ritual and communal engagement with them. How lost are we, I've sometimes thought, when our most agreed-upon ritual now is Halloween, in which we march our children through the streets in store-bought costumes in quest of Hershey's Kisses, while the Mexicans, that same weekend each year, are in cemeteries by candlelight laying marigolds at the tombs of the dead?

In *The Labyrinth of Solitude*, the great Mexican poet and essayist Octavio Paz explained the deeper significance of communal ritual in his nation: "If we make ourselves anonymous in daily life, in the whirlwind of the Fiesta, we let go. We don't just open up: we tear ourselves open. Song, love, friendship: it all ends in howling and tearing." I glimpsed something of this, entirely by accident, at the Checkerboard Club in Chicago. "The explosive and dramatic, sometimes suicidal way in which we lay ourselves bare and yield ourselves up," Paz continues, "almost helpless, reveals how something stifles and inhibits us. Something impedes our being. And because we dare not or cannot confront our being, we revert to the Fiesta."

Paz, being accustomed to the Fiesta, took Mexican stiflement as the interesting point. I, being accustomed to the absence of anything resembling Fiesta—beyond, I don't know, a shopping spree—find that its great, shared uplift and downswing of sorrow is what intrigues.

Rationalism was meant to diminish fear, but ultimately, it has managed to do nothing of the sort; instead it invalidated meaning, which merely served to heighten our dread.

When Murderers Scream at Spiders

And holy to his dread is that dark
Which will neither promise nor explain.

—W. H. AUDEN, "THE AGE OF ANXIETY"

M Y ANXIETY is a shape-shifter. It visits me in unfamiliar guises. Phobias, in particular, tend to take me
by surprise, as they rear up and then fade away depending
upon the stresses in my life. One minute, I'll be going about
my business, being the sort of person who likes to fly on airplanes and to marvel at the deceptive fluffiness of clouds, and
the next thing I know I'm in a state of white-knuckled panic
as the jet I've just boarded powers itself off the tarmac. After
a few years, that phobia resolves and something else—some
other act or object—unexpectedly becomes the embodiment of all that is terrifying.

At the moment, there is an envelope on my dining room
table that fills me with more discomfiture than any other threat
I can conceive of short of standing on the edge of a cliff. The
mailman delivered it two weeks ago, and the envelope has been

very quietly and persistently menacing me ever since. I've taken to serving dinner in the kitchen and answering the phone upstairs. At night, lying in bed, I think about the envelope and feel flooded with a cold Atlantic wave of dire prospect. Penury awaits; I know this. Penury, jail time, unspecified explosions, and a variety of damning conclusions about my character.

I wouldn't be surprised if there were physical dimensions, as yet undiscovered by our scientists, in which one could hear the envelope on my dining room table hiss or tick. Tick, tick, tick . . . Possibly, in those other dimensions, it is even giving off a pulsing, irradiated glow of green. Nevertheless, here in Rational World, all I can tell you for certain is that the envelope is return-addressed from *Revenu Québec*. It is a tax bill.

Where phobia is concerned, to *each their own*, as they say. Mine is an idiosyncratic terror, but so is paledophobia, the fear of bald people, and asymmetriphobia, the fear of asymmetrical things. In their beguiling individuality, phobias are the territory of Oliver Sacks, the neurologist and author who writes about how minds are uniquely molded. Consider, for instance, a story that the BBC aired in England recently about a woman who had grown terrified of peas. After the birth of her daughter, Louise Arnold developed an embarrassing and unmanageable terror of the vegetable. "I've got to stop this," she told the press, "because I can't bear to be in the same room as peas. There have been occasions where I've been out for a meal and asked the waiter for no peas and had to rush out of the restaurant when they forget. I can't even go to my local pub because they serve peas on the menu. I'd love to lead a normal life and be able to go into the pub and have a drink."

"Sometimes," Nicky Lidbetter of Britain's National Phobics Society told the BBC's correspondent, "when people are at a difficult point in their lives, their subconscious attaches the stress they experience to something, like peas." Well, certainly, to peas. Why not? I have seen a grown man run shrieking from a basket of peaches. I have watched a woman grow pale and short of breath in the presence of a clown. In parts of Asia there is the phenomenon of koro, characterized by the suffocating suspicion that one's penis is very slowly shrinking and being reabsorbed by one's body. In south India, people have been known to develop the terror that they're pregnant with a litter of puppies.

When the BBC ran their story, they received a number of posts to their Web site. "I have an incredible fear of boats," one man allowed. "It's silly and irrational and I realise that, but the bigger the ship, the more terrified I am of the thought of it floating on water or even going out to sea." Wrote another: "I have a terrible fear of birds, feathers, and anything with wings. Walking around town squares in Europe is frightening and hellish for me—the thousands of pigeons seem like brainless assassins after my life."

"I am terrified of scarecrows," posted Matt from Kent. "I just find them truly hideous to behold." Admitted Nadia of Brighton: "I have a phobia of flamingos. If one comes on the television I normally retch." Someone else described their phobia of gravy, which my husband would relate to; I have it in my power to drive him from the house with a jar of Hellmann's mayonnaise. At first, years ago, I actually tried to analyze the significance of his reaction to pale-hued condiments. Gradually, however, I came to believe that the object, itself, possesses little relevance beyond its totemic power to contain fear.

Phobia is a coping mechanism. If people who feel disturbed by the prospect of pandemic influenza can devote hours and hours to "hypothetical analytical planning" in order to stave off catastrophe, it is equally probable that one can cope with anxiety by containing it within or assigning it to a single object. Instead of ensnaring threats in a net of facts and plans, one simply allots them a definable location that can be *run away* from. *All that I fear is contained in a pea.*

I recently went to see Dr. Stéphane Bouchard, a National Research Council fellow who is one of the world's leading experts on phobia. Bouchard, a trim, casually attired man who looks a little like the actor Kevin Spacey, works out of a rambling wooden house on the campus of the Université du Québec in Gatineau, a short drive from Ottawa. His second-floor office is filled with gadgets, virtual reality goggles—which he uses for exposure therapy—and a plastic cross-secton model of the human brain.

"One third of phobics," he said, "have had an actual experience with what they fear. So, this is conditioning, or vicarious learning." Also known in the literature as traumatic phobia. An example might be a fear of dogs based on being bitten, or having seen someone else snarled at or attacked. (About 6 percent of North Americans have an "incapacitating" fear of animals.) In terms of my bills phobia, it might be argued that the initial trauma was the day that a man who would only identify himself as "Mr. Hobbs" called me about a forgotten American Express bill while I was breast-feeding my newborn son. He then phoned my neighbor Bob, hassled Ambrose at work, and had his supervisor threaten to put me in jail unless I marched over to a Money Mart, *right now*, presumably with my nursing bra still flapping open. All this, Mr. Hobbs did in twenty-four hours. It was incredibly aggressive and jarring. Not to mention illegal. And ever after, this fear of bills.

Bouchard continues: "Another third of phobics hear about something, like a plane crash or a shark attack, and make a link between that information and an unknown yet perceived threat." Here, I think of my daughter, developing her apprehensiveness about a stranger coming through the window shortly after she heard about an abducted child— hers being a solitary version, I guess, of everyone in America developing an irrational anxiety about serial killers, which journalists like me helped inflame. Shark phobias rose sharply after *Jaws* came out. God knows what the current crop of horror films is doing. Certainly, we are seeing an increase in weather-related phobias. Professors at the University of Texas in Austin reported in 2005 that their new students from California were all petrified of tornadoes, even though they hadn't shown any overt concern about earthquakes in their own state.

"Then, with one third," Dr. Bouchard concluded, shrugging, "we don't have a clue where it comes from." My cousins are all terrified of the submerged trees known as deadheads in the bay at their childhood cottage, which they came to call "The Logs." To this day, none of them can approach The Logs without a heightened sense of dread. An evolutionary psychologist might say that in their very still and lurking posture, The Logs resemble crocodiles and other ancient enemies.

Aaron Beck, the founding director of the Center for Cognitive Therapy in Philadelphia, has done research suggesting that phobias manifest themselves according to psychological themes. For example, a fear of social rejection would be one theme, and might assume the guise of anxiety about public speaking or of being in crowds. In North America, this kind of phobia typically involves a fear of being scorned or humiliated, whereas in Asia, it involves a fear of giving offense, so it might materialize as a phobia of body odor, or using a public washroom. Other themes that Beck identifies have to do with moving through spaces—heights, bridges, dark forests, caves—or with injury and bleeding. "These findings," Beck says, "indicate that a person

who fears height is likely to also fear tunnels but not necessarily being ignored."

Beck also describes the phenomenon of "spreading
phobias"—where an initial fear cascades into several others,
"the linkage being the similarity in consequences or danger
rather than in the objects" themselves. You watch *Jaws* and
develop a phobia of sharks. The horror spreads to baths and
swimming pools and finally to water in general. Toward the
end of my sojourn as a crime journalist, my phobias spread
like a madness. At the family cottage, the one where my
heart had been broken years earlier, I found myself unable to
sleep, so frightened did I feel about the quiet forest dark. I
took to arming myself with a kitchen knife, tucked under
the mattress just in case. I was phobic of predators, both animal and human. I could not step outside the cottage after
nightfall without a juddering, heart-thudding sense of alarm.
In the ensuing years, as my life grew more peaceful and solid
beneath my feet, these menaces entirely receded.

People can have the same phobias for completely different
underlying reasons. A fear of flying, for instance, can relate to
acrophobia (fear of heights), or to claustrophobia (fear of
confined spaces), or to a displaced and more profoundly
threatening anxiety, as in the case of a friend of mine whose
grief and anxiety after his mother died manifested itself as
a phobia of air travel. Similarly, people can have multiple and
apparently distinct phobias that are, in fact, connected by a

common underlying theme. Beck cites the case of a man who "feared going through swinging doors, driving his car, and disclosing business secrets." It emerged that "the common denominator" in these scenarios was that "he feared he might harm someone, either directly or indirectly."

Last year, Clara made a sock puppet, to which she affixed about thirty of the little black-and-white googly eyes you can buy at a craft store. She called the puppet "Aliena." Her father thought it brilliantly imaginative and assigned Aliena pride of place on his desk. Every time I walked into Ambrose's office, I would stumble across the puppet and have to look wildly away, lifting up my arm to shelter my gaze. "The eyes! Those eyes! Good lord!"

Clusters seem to disgust me. Not flocks—I don't mind hordes of birds or bats. When my Sheltie scoots after the pigeons in the park and they take to the air, I do not, personally, experience them as "brainless assassins after my life." No, it's the vision of witless and aggressive reproduction that I find unnerving. Dandelions, mushrooms, googly eyes. Buzz off with the mindless profusion. I can't stand that sense of things just . . . popping up all over the place. This is a subject of great interest to the scholar William Miller, author of *The Anatomy of Disgust*. There are horrors that have more to do with disgust than with fear, although the two emotions are closely intermingled. What disgusts us isn't necessarily something we feel is going to harm us—we just want to distance ourselves, to recoil. We don't want what Miller calls "thick, greasy life" to be *on* us, or *in* us. Certain substances raise the prospect of contamination or invasion. "The disgusting can possess us," says Miller, "fill us with creepy, almost eerie feelings of being not quite in control." Hence, some people's aversions to mayonnaise and gravy and pond scum or, in my case, to multiplying clusters.

Another aspect of the disgusting that Miller contemplates has to do with the partibility of the human body. The body can be pulled apart. Drawn and quartered. Loosened by decay. Few things are more disgusting in one's mouth than a human hair, because it signifies this bodily disintegration. Miller cites a study in which toddlers were observed placing all manner of unlikely objects in their mouths; they were happy to eat poo and paint and other odds and ends, but showed aversion to a single strand of hair. On this point, Miller challenges Freud about his analysis of "castration fear." It isn't just the penis men fear losing, Miller argues, but also their fingers and toes. A classic anxiety dream features the crumbling of one's teeth. We fear *falling apart*.

It is interesting that the two diseases most intensely feared in recent history have been cancer and leprosy. One evokes that nameless dread of aggressive, unpredictable invasion or spread; the other speaks to the horror of partibility. (Consider that during the time of European leper colonies, everyone was riddled with infectious disease of one kind or another, but only the lepers were shunned.)

The British historian Joanna Bourke likewise points out that "cancer phobia" is a phenomenon that has really flared up in the last century. In 1896, according to her research, "when people were asked what disease they feared, only 5 percent named cancer, while between a quarter and a third drew attention to the scary nature of each of the following ailments: smallpox, lockjaw, consumption and hydrophobia." (The latter being the advanced stages of rabies.) "In the fear stakes," Bourke continues, "being crushed in a rail accident or during an earthquake, drowning, being burned alive, hit by lightning, or contracting diphtheria, leprosy or pneumonia all ranked higher than cancer."

Fifty years later, 70 percent of respondents in one British survey identified cancer as their greatest fear. Very few people, by contrast, fear the heart disease and car accidents that are as likely to kill them. "Part of the pervasive anxiety about cancer," Bourke speculates, "was related to the invisibility of a 'cause.'" Cancer was, and is, a specter that stalks us without reason. That is something that Westerners in particular find highly alarming.

In general, women have more phobias than men. Two thirds of animal phobics are women, even though they're no more likely to be stung, gored, or bitten than men. (Mind you, I recently discovered that T. S. Eliot shared my phobia of cows, which I found to be quite thrillingly consoling.) I asked Stéphane Bouchard why this might be. "We don't have a clear answer," he told me. "Usually, we raise little girls to be more aware of their emotions, and they seem to become more sensitive to messages from the amygdala. You see it in brain scans. It's also possible that society is more permissive toward women's avoidance behaviors. Men are forced to

work through their anxieties because avoidance is less toler-
ated in them. More men than women consult with therapists
about social phobia, for this same reason."

It is certainly the case that phobias can be worked
through, although that may simply mean that one's anxiety
shifts to a different place. Some phobias are simply more *in
the way*, as it were, and need resolving. I can fear cows until
they come home; it doesn't really matter unless I work on a
ranch. But I had to get over my fear of flying because I
needed to travel, so I continued to fly, availing myself each
time of a handful of those mini bottles of wine the flight at-
tendants sell, until one day I noticed that the fear had gone. I
had paid no attention to the plane taking off and remained
absorbed in the novel I was reading. The key, very simply,
was exposure, and the tool used by Bouchard and other psychologists for this purpose is a chair and a pair of virtual reality goggles.

"The aim of virtual reality therapy," he explains, "is to
change the association between the stimuli and the threat. In
VRT, you just need enough stimuli to trigger the emotional
part of the brain to make it credible. The quality of VR en-
vironments sucks. But it doesn't matter to the phobic. It's
a really fast emotional process. See these black cables?" He
motions to some equipment cables coiling around the floor
near his desk. "The shape and color will go to the amygdala
and trigger an anxious response in a snake phobic before the
information goes to the prefrontal lobe."

He's right, it's fascinating: if I look at the graphics provided for Virtual Thunderstorm or Virtual Airplane, I am merely interested and even faintly amused by how rudimentary the scenery looks. But Virtual Heights instantly provokes a swooning sense of vertigo. Suddenly, the aesthetics are irrelevant. I have the actual, bodily sensation of falling (which is known as "somatic imaging"). My first memory of being acutely afraid of heights dates to 1978, when my mother took me to New York to visit my father, who was working at the United Nations and living (when not at home with us on weekends) in the diplomat-infested Beekman Towers on the East Side. Everything, of course, was vivid about my first trip to New York: my first time inhaling the toasty fragrance of roasted pretzels in the autumn air, a walk through Central Park at dusk, a Broadway show, and my first visit to the World Trade Center, opened five years earlier and still an exciting new tourist site. *Have you been up the towers?*

I remember peering through the floor-to-ceiling glass from the restaurant at the top of the World Trade Center, down at the Hudson River a thousand-odd feet below, and feeling momentarily overcome with the impulse to jump. What *if?* What if I jumped? What if I pushed myself through the transparent, barely there glass and with one, determined lunge abandoned myself forever? Watching people leap from the World Trade Center on September 11 evoked such an intense sympathetic response in me that I buckled at the knees.

The element of somatic imaging in certain phobias—in which you feel the sensation of falling, or the claustrophobic sensation of airless choking, is a testament to how powerfully our imaginations engage in these fears. People with blood phobias have an empathetic, physiological response to pictures in which they see others bleeding. They can faint, apparently as an unconscious reaction to the prospect of blood loss, since our bodies will stave off further bleeding by inhibiting activity through prompting us to black out. A 1984 study of blood phobics confirmed that when phobics were shown images of someone else's gory injury, they experienced a sharp drop in heart rate and blood pressure, and around 25 percent actually passed out.

Unfortunately, Dr. Bouchard and his colleagues have yet to develop a virtual environment featuring Québec tax officials handing out statements, reminder notices, and threats to garnishee my wages. For this exposure work, I turn to a psychologist who specializes in Cognitive Behavioral Therapy. Over the last few weeks, the psychologist—I'll call him Dave—has handed me an array of assignments. To practice opening envelopes, to look at my ATM receipts before tossing them away like live grenades, and to imagine a scenario in which I run plumb out of cash. Flat out. What, Dave wants to know, is the worst thing you can imagine that would happen?

The aim of Dave's exercise is to find out why I feel like I cannot cope. Being a professional writer, it is relatively easy for me to script something that is vivid for him to read, but not truly all that threatening to me, and he knows it. After I first create a scenario in which, having no cash, I sell my house and move to the boreal forest to start a sustainable living community, he gently scolds me, and makes me do it again. What is so *threatening* here, Patricia? Obviously something is, or I would open my bills and balance my checkbook and track my payments like a normal person.

An element of the phobic response is this fear that one cannot cope. In other words, we don't only quiver at the stimulus, we shrink back from the prospect that we cannot handle the stimulus. Or, more to the point, the stimulus reminds us of our more broadly abiding sense that we cannot manage life's challenges. "The center cannot hold," as Yeats wrote.

"I go to the bank machine," I reimagined the scenario for Dave. "It advises me that I don't have any funds. I don't know why I have no funds since I cannot keep track of the money that ebbs and flows into my account the way it does for all freelancers, piling in from big payouts and then getting sucked out almost at once by staved-off debts. Right away, I am reminded that this is the problem: I don't *know* where my money has gone. I am not in control of this money. This sparks the further, scorching reminder that I am not in control of my life. There was a time, in the bright and hopeful days of my twenties, when I didn't care that I had no control over money because, one day, I would. But that's not what happened. There is no longer a 'one day' motif in my thinking. The day is now, and I am screwed."

I take the scenario back to the psychologist. "How's this?" I ask.

"Better," he says, but only after I read it aloud and tears begin to glisten in my eyes. He's made me hit a nerve. He watches me closely now, I can see the quickened interest in his eyes. He asks me whether it matters if I am in control, or what it is exactly I think that I mean about being in control. Maybe I could try to be more flexible about my expectations, more open to letting life lead me along unanticipated routes and paths.

It is misleading to think that phobias are irrational in that what is feared is inherently silly or harmless. There is nothing irrational, per se, about fearing poverty. But what Aaron Beck has stressed is that in the phobic response, "cognitive distortions, visual imagery, and somatic imagery combine to magnify the actual danger." In the fear of flying, for example, someone not planning a trip in the near future might estimate "the chance of a plane crash as 1:100,000." But, as soon as that person has an actual flight scheduled, his estimated probabilities of a crash increase dramatically. "By the time the airplane started to take off, he would figure the chances as 50:50. If the trip was bumpy, the odds would switch over to 100:1 in favor of a crash."

Exposure to the feared stimulus quells phobia in a manner that reasoned argument never does. Here, I wish to quote at length from a letter that my cousin sent me about his efforts to reason with his phobias of The Logs and other cottage-bound things: "Our family cottage is unsurpassed in sheer quantity of lurking places," he mused. "You know what I'm talking about. You remember lying awake, paralyzed in the bunkie, all alone, or worse yet, all alone with a dog who growls every time a vole walks over a leaf. My dog Sam and I spent many hours in the bunkie, growling and quivering respectively at the sounds of voles, convinced that they were really the sounds of crazed axe murderers trying to sound like voles.

"I have grown out of that fear and can spend perfectly restful nights alone now," he added. "And even though I still get those old pangs of dread as I approach the dark basement, complete with its creaky door, they are something I can overcome with a little internal discourse that resolves itself before I reach out for the doorknob. It's an ongoing grudge match between rationality and neurosis. One such dialogue might start with the simple argument that a door that creaks contains no more evil than a nice quiet one. This logic, I rebut, simply eliminates creakiness as a criteria for evil in a basement door and only results in a fear of all basement doors regardless of their creakiness—an uppercut to the chin of rationality. Pulling itself off the mat after that blow and with time running out, rationality counters with a sucker punch of its own. Eschewing logic for sheer impact it goes for the old 'Don't be such a baby!' approach. TKO for rationality. The preposterousness of a grown man being afraid of his own basement is a compelling thing."

Carl Jung felt that the ultra-rational modern man was doomed to have the unconscious rise up and seize him by the ankle, regardless of all his punctilious and tidy argumentation. In his writings on this subject, Jung noted the case of his patient who was suffering from cancer phobia. This man,

Jung said, "forced everything under the inexorable law of reason, but somewhere nature escaped and came back with a vengeance." Indeed, it has been observed by some psychologists interested in cross-cultural research that the more a culture insists upon rational control, the more it will tend to generate anxiety, because it is that much more fearful of *losing* control.

The American composer Allen Shawn, in his memoir *Wish I Could Be There: Notes from a Phobic Life*, describes an existence completely devoted to maintaining control, but in a manner that winds up being manifestly irrational. Shawn suffers from agoraphobia, an anxiety so narrowly assigned to the matter of unfamiliar spaces that he can happily teach, perform on the piano, entertain friends, and write books, but he cannot walk along a railway track near his home on a pleasant afternoon without carrying a cell phone, some tranquilizers, and a paper bag in which to breathe.

What is striking about Shawn's descriptions of his phobia are the rituals he has devised to enable him to maintain illusory control. "Sometimes," he writes, "I keep a log on a yellow pad next to me on the drive to a new place, to help me cope with my experience . . . noting everything I pass furnishes me with a kind of Ariadne's thread for the return trip." In other words, this accomplished musician, the son of legendary *New Yorker* editor William Shawn, who was himself agoraphobic, cannot drive from A to B on a bucolic road in rural Vermont without writing down, "Quail Hollow Inn, Yankee Pet Supply, Cold River Industrial Park, Chuck's

Auto . . ." and every other sign he comes across, lest he collapse in a total panic.

What would have happened to intelligent, erudite, and frankly privileged men like Allen and William Shawn—safely affluent and well-connected in a peaceful corner of the world in postwar America—if they'd been forced to flee pell-mell from war or tornado, without access to their pens? Would these two revered men have run off screaming and jabbering? More likely, in the crush of real events they would have realized that uncharted side roads in Vermont or New York City were not that menacing, after all, and that more challenging prospects were at hand.

When my friend Julia, who works for the British government as a health policy advisor in Zimbabwe, hears about my research for this book, she grows visibly impatient and disdainful. She is raising children in a country where the currency is in free fall, where regularly people discover themselves to be destitute overnight, or learn of relatives who've just been shot in the head. Within the realm of that kind of chaos, she demands, who the hell has time to jot down Quail Hollow Inn or its local African equivalent? What people have time to do is deal with the real hazards, for which all this other stuff is just fancy and convenient displacement. From Julia's point of view, the reason that anxiety disorder rates are lower in parts of Africa, and highest globally in the United States, is because Africans are actually dealing with the catastrophe of death and poverty and loss. It's all right there in their faces. Who needs displacement?

She has a point, but it's not quite that straightforward. Coping strategies, through the use of ritual, superstition, and even highly somatic experiences, remain pervasive. Nigerians, for instance, may have been deemed to be some of the happiest people in the world in spite of their challenges, but they also suffer to a significant degree from a culture-bound form of hysteria known as sleep paralysis. Sufferers of this experience will wake up in the middle of the night and find themselves completely stifled and unable to move. The feeling is understood as being ridden by a demon or a witch. Variations on this theme of being cursed or bound or transfixed by sorcery abound throughout Africa. A recipe or counterspell is then called for, and often purchased at markets.

In Cambodia, in the aftermath of the vast collective trauma inflicted by the Khmer Rouge, people continue to experience panic attacks, which are interpreted as being "hit by the wind." The sufferer's skin pores have opened too much, it is thought, and therefore the body has grown vulnerable to invasions from wind, causing shortness of breath and other physical symptoms that we Westerners interpret as panic. Again, a recipe is called for: a friend or relative uses coins to calmly and methodically draw the wind from the pores of the sufferer. And this idea—this conviction—that something is being done to restore calm to the situation actually does produce calm.

There is little overt difference between the behavior involved in warding off the impact of trauma in these highly idiosyncratic, culture-bound ways and the strict ritualized behavior that characterizes what we call obsessive-compulsive disorder.

The anthropologist Robert Lemelson interviewed people with OCD on the Indonesian island of Bali, to see how their behavior was mirroring cultural beliefs. One of his subjects, named Pak Balik, was obsessed with knowing the names of everyone he encountered in the street. He carried a notepad with which to jot down their names, or at very least their license plates. "Like, if I saw someone else outside, I had a feeling that I 'must know' him or her," he explained to the anthropologist. It emerged that Balik had survived a massacre in his village during the coup against former president Sukarno. Traumatized, he set about keeping his oceanic feelings at bay by inventing these small rituals of mastery.

Another of Lemelson's subjects, Pak Gede Sudiasih, a forty-four-year-old man who worked for the government, had also lived through the coup, and felt compelled to investigate dead chickens that he saw along the roadside on his way to the office. He told Lemelson, "If I'm riding my bicycle to work and I see a dead chicken lying by the side of the road, I have to stop and look at it. When I get back on my bicycle and ride a hundred yards, I get this feeling that I need to look at it again. I think, 'Well, what color was its head?' So I return and look at its head." He would repeat this process several times, until he had thoroughly reviewed the various colors of the chicken, and then he would arrive late for work. Pak Sudiasih also needed, compulsively, to check on the names of people who passed by his house. "If he could not find out their names," says Lemelson, "he felt so anxious that he wanted to die." Psychologists have observed that patients engaged in anxiety-allaying rituals are relatively fine so long as they are not interrupted. I thought back to my year in Chicago, and how my anxiety worsened because my graduate work kept interrupting me from my ritual of 'hypothetically, analytically' solving the mathematical equation of my rejection.

Lemelson makes the point that OCD symptoms differ from culture to culture, as phobia does, acting as a lens that magnifies what preoccupies the society as a whole. Orthodox Jews in Israel who display OCD symptoms, he notes, do so by way of engaging in "over-analysis of religious questions and doubting." A number of Arab Muslims with OCD symptoms, on the other hand, grow obsessed with religiously inflected themes of impure thoughts and contaminations, while their compulsions mirror their normal religious rituals, featuring the five daily prayers that have to be done, facing in a particular direction, always uttering a specific sequence of words. Not surprisingly, they are less likely than secular OCD sufferers to realize that they even have a problem. Maybe they don't. Their rituals absorb their anxiety collectively, as suggested in one study of Egyptian adolescents with clinically identified OCD, who were not found to have any significant "co-morbid anxiety disorders," meaning they did not also suffer panic disorder, generalized, anxiety disorder, or any phobias. Left to their daily remonstrations, they were in healthy frames of mind.

A couple of years ago, I was asked to review the eminent British scientist Richard Dawkins's book *The God Delusion*. I preface any further comment by saying that I am not a devoted churchgoer, but my faith has certainly been evolving. I've followed Tolstoy on his wending path, and Marcus Aurelius, and C. S. Lewis and Elie Wiesel and a host of other thinkers and writers who offer nuanced insights into the human condition. Sitting on my couch with my morning coffee and *The God Delusion*, I found my respect for Dawkins steadily diminishing as I turned the pages and encountered a kind of spittle-inflected zealotry in support of the rational mind. His avid followers would disagree, I know, but by dismissing Thomas Aquinas as "infantile," other theologians as "fatuous," and suggesting that Jesus Christ was "honestly mistaken" when he claimed to be the son of God, Dawkins was asking me to do something easy and impetuous. Flip the bird at religion! As if my culture hadn't been goading me to do that since I entered adulthood. As if it was a radically new enticement.

By focusing his disdain entirely on the violence done in God's name, Dawkins misses a few important points, the most significant one being how and why both the need for deeper meaning and spiritual ritual are so important in human life.

One of Karla Homolka and Paul Bernardo's adolescent victims, Kristen French, was from a religious family, who drew deep comfort from their faith. They were anchored in a similar way to the Pennsylvania Amish who responded to the shooting death of five of their children in a schoolhouse in 2006 by visiting the widow of the murderer right away and assuring her that her husband was forgiven. Unquestionably, the great religions have recognized and responded to this human need for consolation and steadying through ritual and mantra. Recalled William James of his period of extreme anxiety, "if I had not clung to scripture-like texts . . . I think I should have grown really insane."

In forgoing the sustaining myths and organizing ethics of religious traditions, as a culture we are not doing a very good job of being purely secular and rational. Where once we feared devils and fell on our knees at the altar, we now engage in random acts of being frightened of peas, or of needing to smoke, to drink, to check on dead chickens, to jot down the shop signs on the road. As Jung pointed out a century ago, rationalism will persistently try but it cannot, ultimately, win out because the human experience is *not* entirely rational.

As I practice bringing my eyes into focus on the small squares of white paper that get spit out by automatic teller machines at the store, I am fully aware that conquering my phobia of financial matters will not conquer my propensity to be anxious. But it will, I hope, vanquish my anxiety to a less complicated corner of my life than the bank. At best, we can all steer our little terrors in this fashion, away from what would actually cause us greater harm.

Fear of Failure, Fear of Success: Anxiety in the Workplace

[Fame] boils down to immortality. I want to live forever. And the best way to live forever is to be better than everyone else. But it's fucking impossible. There's beautiful artists die every day, and never get recognized.

—DAMIEN HIRST

I ONCE GOT thrown out of a restaurant in midtown Manhattan by an infuriated television executive before the entrées had even arrived. I found myself standing on the sidewalk on Seventh Avenue in the late June light in a daze, and began walking through Central Park in absentminded pursuit of a hot pretzel as a substitute for the exciting Italian pasta dish I'd ordered about ten minutes earlier; the adrenaline of the knockdown was still buzzing through my brain.

The year was 1992, and I was field-producing the show *Confessions of Crime*. The two former *Hard Copy* producers who worked with me had suddenly been fired. They were good at their jobs, which is to say they were proficient at luring the unwary before the camera, but they didn't get along with one of the executive producers, the bucktoothed British one who'd sung backup for 10cc. He couldn't stand the way they reminded him that his life was a farce, or something along those lines; my memory isn't clear.

In any event, they were fired, and they plotted revenge. They snuck back into our office over a weekend and stole the interview notes and research material from my desk so that we couldn't film our next episode. It was silly spite straight out of high school, only with many thousands of dollars on the line.

That night, the network producer overseeing our show had convened an emergency dinner meeting at Trattoria Dell'Arte, a large and rather clamorous restaurant filled with mirrors, frescoes, and frantic waitstaff. "*Why* didn't she lock up her files?" the network exec demanded of the buck-toothed Brit, referring to me without deigning to address me directly. I volunteered an answer, risking further wrath by daring to appear in the executive's midst as an embodied human presence: "I'm sorry. I didn't know you were going to fire them, and . . . but . . . even if I had known, I didn't expect that they would steal stuff from my desk."

At this, the executive turned her glare on me full force, and then abruptly pounded the table so aggressively that the cutlery jumped: "Wake up! This is *television*!" She glared at me for a long, strange moment, and then returned her attention to my boss: "I'm finished with her, she needs to leave."

The way I view it now, I traded my entrée for two enduring lessons about life. Number one: Stay the hell away from television. It appears to have developed a God complex. Number two: To the best of your ability, skirt the edges of what has come to be known, in business books and magazines, as "the toxic workplace." We are very much taken up in this culture with the concept of stress: work is stressful, home is stressful, life is stressful. But stress is a bit of a red herring. Being extremely busy is not precisely the same stress as living through the Great Depression or the world wars. What stresses us is not what or how much we do, but how we interpret the significance of our acts. And right now, quite acutely, we are beset by self-doubt.

According to a 2006 survey conducted by the Anxiety Disorders Association of America, many Americans are experiencing an extreme amount of stress and anxiety in their daily work lives; nearly half of them report "persistent or excessive anxiety." Why should this be? Is it a variant of the neurologist George Beard's nineteenth century concept of "American nervousness"? Possibly, but there are some particularly modern challenges involved. The greatest of these is job insecurity. Many corporations have no loyalty; they engage in the relentless manufactured cheer of "team building" and then drop you like a stone if you have to do something inconveniently human, like care for an ailing father. The disconnect between their backslapping efforts to make you a part of their happy team and their brutal disregard for your personal life can be downright scary. A friend of mine described the remorselessness with which he got fired from a happy, patriotic, Olympic-team-supporting clothing company: "It was like getting whacked." A mafia hit. That fast, decisive, and impersonal. Another friend was let go via e-mail, and he wouldn't have been the only one. At least he wasn't escorted out of the office on the spot by security guards.

Between 2001 and 2004, approximately 3.5 million Americans disappeared altogether from the labor force, many of them—according to management professors Sherry Sullivan and Lisa Mainiero—being seasoned professionals in their forties and fifties who simply could not find new work at their level of expertise. Sullivan and Mainiero quote the management consultant Peter Drucker: "There is no longer any corporate ladder. There isn't even a rope ladder. It's more like a jungle, and you bring your own machete."

Men, arguably, are especially vulnerable to these frightening and casual rejections, because their core self-esteem is more bound up in career accomplishment than family life. For some, the depth of dread involved in being "whacked" would not be dissimilar to what I felt when my lover tossed me out before I went to Chicago. Such men feel a distress that's profound. Some have breakdowns. I have seen it several times, and in different professions. They silently experience what my friend echoed back to me from his journal, the panic that you cannot show.

For women, anxiety in relation to work tends to have more diffuse sources. A consistent disparity in wages and promotions is obviously still generating anguish. To realize that your education, talent, and drive cannot ultimately reward you as much as the shape of your genitalia is a harsh, disorienting truth. When we are young, we're encouraged to believe that "grrls rule." But they don't. As Sullivan and Mainiero write, "women are persistently excluded from the social decision-making networks, making it difficult, if not impossible, for them to be considered major players in the workplace." Visit a bookstore, and you'll see titles in the business section that sound almost desperate: *The Art of War for Women* or *Hardball for Women* or *The Corporate Dominatrix*. In last year's advice book *Am-BITCH-ous*, author Debra Condren offers women a set of rules to play by to get what they deserve at the office. One of her rules: "Be more irresponsible to others—and more responsible to yourself."

What if I say no? No, I will not be more irresponsible to others. I will not steal stuff from their desks, and I won't throw them out of restaurants. That is not a world in which I chose to live. But what, for many of us, is the alternative? According to the ADAA survey, less than half of the Americans experiencing anxiety at work have talked to their employer about it, due to apprehensions about being called "weak," or out of concern that the disclosure would affect their prospects for promotion.

This is a time when the spoils go to the perky, to the relentlessly confident and self-promoting. It is a significant disadvantage to be wary of the spotlight. The truth of this prevails through the hotel conference room where pitches are made or PowerPoints given, on YouTube and Facebook, at meetings, during team-building exercises, and in the sneakier realm of the office. Several recent studies have confirmed that workers who exhibit "neuroticism," in the parlance of business psychologists referring to anxiety, are harder-pressed to gain a promotion, or even a salary increase.

This is not because their *work* is less accomplished. On the contrary, a 2005 study "Can Worriers Be Winners?" concluded that people of "high cognitive ability" who worried and fretted and fussed with their projects ultimately produced better results. That doesn't strike me as surprising. I am thinking of a friend who runs her own company and is frequently up half the night ruminating, or another friend whose perfectionism borders on autism in its narrowness of concentration. Several businesspeople I've seen engage in something very close to OCD. We all know people like this who are brilliant and skilled. So it isn't the measurable impact of "neuroticism" that companies are reacting to when they pass over the anxious and depressed in their decisions about promotions. It is the *appearance* of the trait: you must not *appear* to be doubtful or uncertain or self-scrutinizing in the marketplace. If you do not behave like "one hell of an entitled son of a bitch," or "a hyperconfident and demanding diva," then carry on doing your excellent work but don't expect applause.

Seventy-nine percent of workers responding to a poll conducted for the Global Business and Economic Roundtable on Addiction and Mental Health in 2007 said they believed a person diagnosed with depression would keep the fact secret to avoid damaging their future opportunities.

About half of those polled believed, further, that someone missing work because they were depressed would be more likely "to get into trouble and maybe even be fired."

Business psychologists, who provide methods of screening and winnowing prospective employees to human resource departments, now speak in terms of "psychological capital." Companies thrive on the basis of their financial capital, their educational or skills capital, and now, apparently, on the basis of their ability to build an extroverted and upbeat workforce, which is their "psychological capital." This notion reminds me of the paintings of bold and happy comrades in the former Soviet Union on display in Moscow museums when my father was posted there in the early 1980s, the so-called socialist realist figures striding across the industrial landscape with pink-cheeked vigor. It's disturbing.

In the spring of 2006, *Managed Care* magazine published a special issue entitled "Depression in the Workplace." The publication advised its readers—mostly benefits managers—about the costs of depression to a company's bottom line. "These indirect costs show up," one expert was quoted as saying, "as absenteeism, poor productivity, flawed decision-making, accidents, turnover, failed projects, faulty products, poor customer service, poor teamwork." Such problems, in turn, "are serious threats to our economic security in a vastly altered competitive landscape." (Whatever that means.) Therefore, HR personnel are advised to screen for this "disease" and offer treatment, such as drugs. (Interesting to note that "Depression in the Workplace" was underwritten by Forest

Laboratories, a company that sells the antidepressants Celexa and Lexapro.)

Mental and emotional problems at work now top physical causes, for the first time, as the primary reason for worker absenteeism. People are not staying home because they have the flu and are afraid of infecting their co-workers, they are staying home when anxiety (or, one assumes, depression) make them unable to face their co-workers or their bosses with a sufficiently chipper demeanor. The snake is eating its tail. Even as our anxiety levels are rising, we feel more stigmatized than ever for revealing ourselves to be anything but what historian Alice Bullard called "the super-competent and self-possessed person of the modern world."

In 1979, the social historian Christopher Lasch famously described America as a "culture of narcissism." The aim in this culture, Lasch argued, is not to be accomplished, but to be noticed; not to perfect one's craft, but to flaunt one's allure. Lasch gained his detractors and his ardent fans, some of whom anticipated the nauseating presence of irradiated media parcels like Paris Hilton. Yet narcissism, at least clinically, is fueled by a deeply felt insecurity, one that drives a person to crave affirmation through attention. That is not how I would characterize the present American culture in general. I think we've proceeded through the pages of the DSM-IV to a state far colder than narcissism.

Fear is one of the pillars that underlies ethics: a fear of

giving offense or of breaking the law, an anxiety about how you make others feel, an apprehension about not being liked. These fears are no longer relevant to success in North American corporate life. Not only is neuroticism punished, but employees are also less likely to be promoted if they have a personality trait identified in such journals as *Personnel Psychology* as "agreeableness." If they are easygoing and warm, happy to do favors and to yield the spotlight, with their identity being bound up in their essential sense of decency and graciousness, rather than their need for power or attention, they will be left in the dust. As one business news headline summed it up: "It doesn't pay to be kind."

No, it doesn't. What is being rewarded in our current culture is a form of pure, self-interested fearlessness that approximates—because it has no ethical dimension—sociopathy. (Hence the popularity of recent books like *The Sociopath Next Door* and *Snakes in Suits: When Psychopaths Go to Work*.) Such is the climate of hucksterism in society now that personal qualities we officially consider disordered and label as "social phobia," "avoidant personality disorder," or "workplace depression" are, in a nation like Japan, merely regarded as good manners. Being deferential, soft-spoken, courteous and self-effacing, experiencing shame—these are essential qualities in Japanese society. "Staring at other people, for example, especially one's elders or superiors, is considered impolite," notes the Princeton scholar Donald Capps. In Japan, "verbal assertiveness and making one's opinion too clear and distinct in public is also regarded as improper," because the society values collaboration over displays of competitive advantage. Capps refers to research done by the Japanese psychiatrist Kenneth Okano, in observing that the kind of "pseudosociophobic" behavior engaged in the high-rise offices of Tokyo (which is to say, business customs that mimic what we would see as social phobia) promotes shame as a virtue. (Not a happy one, necessarily. The turbulence in Japan's economy over the last decade has led to a striking number of suicides.) Nevertheless, the Japanese have a long-held belief that true strength is concealed strength, an understanding of human dynamics that, Capps argues, is echoed in early Christian thought as well but has been lost or forgotten in contemporary American life.

In America, there is no shame in shamelessness. No shame need be felt about behaving badly or rudely, for "there's no such thing as bad publicity." If you want to flash your vagina to photographers in the manner of Britney Spears, or slander everything that moves in the spirit of Ann Coulter, feel free. What is paramount is that you sell yourself by grabbing attention. In fact, more than being paramount as a method of sale, salesmanship has become paramount as a measure of worth: if you do *not* stick your thumb in your mouth and blow up your head to gigantic proportions, people think there's something wrong with your product. They cannot imagine that your work, in itself, is any good, if you're unwilling or unable to behave like Donald Trump in promoting the sale. In arse-backward fashion, the actual intrinsic value of your talent, your craft, your skill at your job is appraised by your level of bravado.

When Melinda Doolittle was voted off *American Idol* before the 2007 final, various pundits speculated that her flaw at the finish line was that she "had no personality." What, I wondered, reading these blogs, is meant by "personality" in such a judgment? Melinda Doolittle was a riveting performer who was also very sweet. I suspect that what was meant by "no personality" was that Doolittle had the temerity—the entirely confusing *nerve*—to be a bit self-effacing.

During the televised auditions for *American Idol*, would-be singers regularly reacted to their rejection by the judges by rearing up and roaring, "Just give me one more chance! Let me sing one more song!" Some accepted their fate, but many were outraged and persistent. This is the kind of egomaniacal behavior we have normalized. The fact that Doolittle just kind of sang her way to the top because she was purely talented was disorienting. Who does she think she is, trying to achieve success through merit while remaining fully aware that she's on America's most successful TV show? What's wrong with her, for being cognizant of that? Or, as judge Simon Cowell chided her at one point in the contest, "Stop acting so surprised."

How is a psychologically healthy adult supposed to react, if not with continued awe and happy surprise, to being favorably responded to on the nation's *most-watched* TV show? Anyone whose answer is "jaded" or "cool as a cucumber" is fully immersed in this culture of sociopathy and needs to be airlifted out, perhaps dropped into some place like the province of Kerala in southern India, where people joyously praise their god for providing a daily tidbit of dinner.

In spite of these prejudices, Americans still abide by the myth that anyone can get ahead through a simple blend of hard work and talent. Because of that lingering romance, they have a difficult time truly believing that success and merit have long since parted ways. In 1961, *Time* magazine ran an essay called "The Age of Anxiety," in which the anonymous author (how modest) pondered the shifting sand beneath our feet. "The most orthodox tenet in the American creed," he or she wrote, "is that the individual can accomplish anything if he tries hard enough. It may be one of the glories of a free society, but it also carries great potential danger . . . From the noble notion that man is free to do anything that he can do, the U.S. somehow subtly proceeds to the notion that he must do anything he can and, finally, that there is nothing he cannot do. This leads to a kind of compulsory freedom that encourages people not only to ignore their limitations but to defy them." Half a century later, the sand has shifted further, and it is the most defiant of all who are successfully positioning themselves at the top.

Consider, by way of example, the nineteen-year-old sophomore at Harvard, Kaavya Viswanathan, who recently won high praise for her amazing debut novel, *How Opal Mehta Got Kissed, Got Wild, and Got a Life*. How exciting that a teen was showing such prodigious talent, in a quintessential tale of overcoming rags (or, at least, immigrant status) and soaring to riches on merit alone! Of course the story turned to discomfiting ashes when it became apparent that this new novel was a hastily cobbled-together pastiche of concepts, clichés, and narrative passages lifted whole cloth from bestselling novels by such authors as Megan McCafferty and Sophie Kinsella. What was striking, though, was that among the mortified young author's peers, her only true transgression was that she was sloppy enough to get caught.

"Around here you've got to be smart, and people know how to manipulate," Chris Lane, a seventeen-year-old former classmate of Viswanathan's, told *USA Today*. "They do whatever it takes to get what they want. She went to an extreme, I guess." Or she was made to believe that such extremes were normal. For this bright young immigrant, the American dream was not about hardscrabble merit, it was manifestly about marketing. She had surely been taught that. Only to be greeted by a horrified and bristling literary community that still has one foot planted firmly in an earlier era. As I write, rumors are circulating on the Internet that the great American writer Jamaica Kincaid has taken Viswanathan under her wing. That appeals to me. I like to think that a girl can struggle back from the craziness she experienced so early in this culture and—having found her voice—offer something real to say.

In the weeks after September 11, a poem by W. H. Auden circulated virally through e-mail across North America. The collective crisis was extreme enough that we reached, for once, to genuine truth in poetry for an articulation of our feelings. What I remember finding interesting, however, was that we had to reach all the way back to Auden, or more specifically to an era when poets were sufficiently revered and respected that they came to serious public attention. People had *heard* of Auden, that is one reason why his poem was being circulated some sixty years later. There are poets now, alive and well, who are creating work of extraordinary beauty. But they are laboring in the silence of small offices. It is more common to hear the phrase "poetry doesn't sell" than to hear anything else at all, really, about contemporary poetry. Are poets, as a category of artist, the first endangered species in an ecosystem of hucksters?

The poet Paul Muldoon relates a very funny story about going to read at a university in upstate New York to an audience of four. The quartet were huddled at the back of the classroom, and had been deep in conversation when Muldoon arrived. Waiting in faint hope for additional listeners, this acclaimed writer eventually decided to go ahead with a selection of verses from his latest collection. His audience smiled politely after the first poem. He began to read a second, but, as he relays, "just before I'd got to the end, one of my fans put up her hand and asked me how long I expected to be. What? The thing was, these students were involved in a study group and had settled in this empty classroom in the hope of finding a little peace and quiet."

If poets are an endangered species in North America, it is arguably because they are the least likely among all of the creative professionals to be *temperamentally* inclined to glad-hand

and cold-call and scheme up sales hooks in promoting their work. Surveying the research on creative intelligence and emotional health, the psychologist Dean Keith Simonton reports that 87 percent of famous poets (for whom we have enough biographical information) can be said to have experienced psychopathology, compared to 28 percent of eminent scientists. By "psychopathology," Simonton is thinking primarily of mood disorders—depression, anxiety, mania.

What does this mean, though? Does it mean that poets are a feebler sort who easily succumb to proverbial attacks of the vapors? Hardly. As Simonton and others have noted, highly creative people have extremely robust ego strength. They couldn't care less what you *think* of them. They are the opposite of Lasch's narcissists. Emily Dickinson was so tormented by anxiety that she could barely leave her house, but her poetry endures because her voice is so authoritative. T. S. Eliot was haunted constantly by depression but expressed himself with the fiery clarity of Martin Luther King Jr. as he denounced the lot of us as "hollow men." William Butler Yeats was a visionary, who also happened to be "painfully turned inwards," according to one of his biographers, Richard Ellmann. Yeats was "totally self-conscious of his own clumsiness and remembered all his life how he felt when Oscar Wilde disapproved of the color of his shoes." He was horrified by social judgment, because he knew the breezing and blowing trends of contemporary fashion weren't his forte, but he could capture the soul spinning within your breast. My grandfather kept a poem by Yeats on his desk in Parliament: "The best lack all convictions [sic], while the worst / Are filled with passionate intensity."

The old saw that genius lies near to madness has some truth to it, although it might be more apt to say that genius lies next to high alarm. Creatively gifted individuals in general are about twice as likely to experience some form of mental distress as "otherwise comparable, noncreative individuals," according to the research. Indeed, one study found that the more eminent the creator, the higher the rate and intensity of his or her symptoms. Simonton writes that "creativity requires the cognitive ability and the dispositional willingness to 'think outside the box'; to explore novel, unconventional, and even odd possibilities; to be open to serendipitous events and fortuitous results; and to imagine the implausible or consider the unlikely. From this requirement arises the need for creators to have such traits as defocused attention, divergent thinking, openness to experience, independence and nonconformity. Let us call this complex configuration of traits the creativity cluster."

And let us say, further, that a person who is headstrong enough to open their eyes and their heart to the full depth and weight of the world is inviting in everything out there—both evil and good, both dark and light—and the sheer bravery of that openness enables them to gain profound insight into the human condition. It also fucks them up. It may even make them more prone to stick their head in an oven than to engage in self-promotional chitchat on Jay Leno.

Among history's most inspired and lasting creators—in art, music, poetry, and prose—a remarkable number were hospitalized for mental illness at one point or another in their lives. Among them, William Faulkner, F. Scott Fitzgerald, Ralph Waldo Emerson, Herman Melville, Eugene O'Neill, Mary Shelley, Robert Louis Stevenson, T. S. Eliot, Leo Tolstoy, Tennessee Williams, Irving Berlin, Noel Coward, Cole Porter, Gustav Mahler, Robert Schumann, Georgia O'Keeffe, and Vincent van Gogh.

It is difficult to return from harrowing experiences with the energy or inclination to formulate a catchy sales pitch for what one has seen. I am not saying that it's impossible for authentically engaged artists to willingly go out afterward and discuss what they've discovered about the world. What I am saying is that most of them would prefer to crawl across broken glass (which in some ways they have) than to pull the kinds of narcissistic, attention-getting stunts at the level that is required in our present era to bring merit into alignment with acclaim. Imagine a man returning from the rough, dark mines of Madagascar with a gem. *That* is what he wishes you to see. Look at the treasure that his toiling has unearthed: look at that, not at him.

The old-style American dream has changed. It has become a mug's game. Once we see that, and start to rethink how to measure ourselves, how to contribute value rather than vanity to our culture, the intense anxiety some feel around work

will likely begin to lessen. This is already beginning to happen: if one form of the American dream is increasingly un-
attainable, a new kind of dream is taking root—one that is
less about a dream in the childlike sense of "I want" and
more about a vision of commitment.

Sullivan and Mainiero talk about an aspect of this in their
book, *The Opt-Out Revolt*, which takes a close-up look at the
roughly eight million Americans who have deliberately
placed themselves out of reach of the corporations, deciding
instead to become independent contractors, consultants, and
freelancers. More men are becoming part-timers and stay-at-
home fathers. More women are starting their own businesses
and pushing back against the corporate dictum to be duplic-
itous, self-centered, and cruel. In their 2006 book, *The Power
of Nice*, ad executives Linda Kaplan Thaler and Robin Koval
detail the ways in which being kind to your colleagues and
employees actually helps your bottom line. They also talk
about the scarce commodity of truth. "In business," they
write, "you often hear about the term 'fake it 'til you make
it.' You're supposed to get in the door with a lot of bluster
and bravado—and *then* figure out what the heck you're doing. We think this is terrible advice." For one thing, your
work will be poor, and for another, if you're not naturally
inclined to be egotistical, the experience is very *anxious-
making*.

Sullivan and Mainiero cite a survey of fifteen thousand
American managers who were asked to select their most
admired leadership qualities. Eighty-seven percent chose

"honesty" amongst their top seven. Perhaps people are tired of being hoaxed, manipulated, bullied, and lied to. Then whacked.

Ever since my brief career in television, I have watched the world of the workplace from the wings, preferring to freelance and often, because of my temperament, avoiding opportunities to promote myself. For many years, I felt quietly aghast with myself for this inability or disinclination, or a blend of the two, to play by the rules of the game. Why could I not be more ballsy, why wasn't I am-bitch-ous, what was wrong with me? Gradually, however, I began to reorient my sense of self-worth and wonder what was wrong with my culture. So I don't get a fancy car and I won't fake it 'til I make it. As Buckminster Fuller has been quoted as saying, "I learned very early and painfully that you have to decide at the outset whether you are trying to make money or make sense." There is surely a way to achieve what you need by being passionate, principled, and self-aware. It is a route that needs taking. What is the alternative? To bolster your shaky confidence with Prozac? Been there, done that—and that is my next cautionary tale.

2001 : A Drugs Odyssey

Bright, energetic, not too serious, not too thoughtful: these qualities are valued in our era of high technology capitalism and the SSRIs seem capable of producing more people in this mold.

—ALICE BULLARD

The antidepressant Catch-22—patients who are needlessly dependent on antidepressants and do not realize it—is a hidden national health crisis.

—JOSEPH GLENMULLEN, HARVARD DEPARTMENT OF PSYCHIATRY

WHEN REASON IS THE ULTIMATE VIRTUE—more prized than honor or courage or faith—there are few places that make one feel quite as deviant as a psychiatrist's waiting room. I am struck by this every time I visit the Centre for Addiction and Mental Health in downtown Toronto, housed in a stern high-rise building next to the University of Toronto campus where I earned my undergraduate history degree. Customarily, I take the elevator up to my psychiatrists's floor, where in addition to his spacious office is a locked ward full of humans who cannot be trusted to behave rationally.

The narrow corridor that leads from the ward to Dr. K. and his colleagues is a liminal space, where I move between worlds. The doctors become noble and elegant and I grow . . . less so. They wear their proverbial white coats, and I metaphorically sport a hospital gown with my bum showing. I can feel the balance of power shift from street level to the fifth floor as if it were a palpable change in air pressure.

Once, during a session with Dr. K., he received an urgent page and had to dart out of his office for a moment. As I sat quietly, sipping my coffee, another psychiatrist entered the room. "May I help you?" he asked, with precisely the same intonation that salesclerks use when they suspect you of shoplifting.

"No, I don't think so," I answered, bemused.

"Well, where is Dr. K.?"

"He's just stepped out for a moment."

"Then," ventured the doctor, "I think you should really wait for him out here in the hall."

I am comforted by the recollections of my friend Peter, now a palaeontologist, who once had a summer job doing housekeeping at his university. He was, he says, quite fascinated by the eccentric state in which he found the dorm rooms when he was cleaning for a group of psychiatrists who were attending a conference. He remembers one who had an alarming number of shoes, all lined up just so against the wall. Another had clothes tossed everywhere, blouses, books, deodorant, personal items thrown about pell-mell, as if the suitcase had exploded. By contrast, Peter says, the bee-keepers who came for a conference were all very tidy and frugal, as if the effort of keeping thousands of angry insects from stinging them every day had bred into them a Zen-like temperament. I was intrigued when Peter made this observation, airily and amiably one night, because psychiatrists have so much invested in appearing to be beekeepers. We are the maddened bees, who buzz into their offices and bang into the window, and they are the Zen masters, cool and still. Sporting a veiled, bee-proof hat. You buzz and wing about and attempt to sting, and they just cross their legs, steeple their fingers, and ask: "Where is this anger coming from?"

"From *you*, you bastard, you just stole my honey!"

Well, in my case, the equivalent exchange one afternoon in the summer of 2002, after I walked into Dr. K.'s office, went like this:

"How could you not have *warned* me of the side effects of Effexor?"

"What side effects?" Steepled hands.

"What *side effects*? I missed a single dose and I felt like I was trapped in a disco club on acid with the strobe light at maximum pulse. I had to veer off from my drive to work and find a pharmacy and beg the pharmacist for *one pill*!"

"You need to calm down," he advised. "Why don't you sit. You have a great deal of anger in you, and you need to think about where it's coming from."

I felt like jutting out my hip the way my teenaged nieces do, and borrowing their heroic contempt: "Uh, duh?"

I was angry at him. So angry that I now fervently related to the movies *One Flew Over the Cuckoo's Nest* and *Frances*, and basically every antipsychiatry screed that has seen print or hit film. Anyone who has ever been on the antidepressant Effexor, or its evil twin Paxil, will know exactly what I am talking about. The question is why weren't we warned?

My experience with drugs begins with the towers falling on 9/11, as is the case for many. I had been free from anxiety, at that time, for six years. Unsurprisingly free, I felt, for my life had grown calm, creative, and fruitful. I'd been married, published books, given birth to Clara and Geoffrey—all endeavors that grounded me profoundly. True, I bought a flashlight and some extra tuna fish before Y2K and had some anxiety bound neatly in parcels by way of ongoing, intermittent phobias. But it was the deepening winter of 2002 when I lost my balance once again, arms aflail. Partly, it had to do with my job. In the harrowing weeks that followed al-Qaeda's attack, I was unable to ignore further headlines—anthrax! the shoe bomber!—because my work as a newspaper columnist obliged me to pay attention to every unnerving development. Then, in mid-December, I had a further shock: the sudden death of a beloved friend, whose cancer had crept through her body, unnoticed, until it was too late. She died on Clara's fifth birthday. At her memorial service in the week before Christmas, we all wept uncontrollably. It was a time of intense and unexpected sorrow.

In modern secular culture, there isn't a Hallmark card on the shelf that manages to console us in times of grief. Friends become tongue-tied. Unable to say, "It's God's will," or "She's in a better place," they are left to stammer out utterly insufficient phrases that don't even begin to encourage healing. "I heard about your friend, that's terrible." Or: "Sorry about what happened." Bummer, man.

My own grief intensified—not only because it was featureless, with no access to a larger narrative—but also because I felt guilt for being unable to console the son and daughter of this friend. I don't mean a shoulder-shrugging sort of guilt, I mean a choking sense of dismay, as if, once again, I had been returned to this precipice of meaninglessness. One night, as Clara lay beside me on her bed, she whispered in the darkness: "Mummy? If I die before you do, I'll watch over you." I'm not sure what prompted her to say that, since I'd been careful not to speak of Mary Anne in front of my daughter, but her faith was the healing balm I needed. If only there were more of it, and the culture that surrounded me wasn't so denuded that the only lesson I was meant to take from Mary Anne's death was that smoking caused cancer.

In February, I read *People* magazine one day in the supermarket, discovered that Carol Burnett's daughter had just died of lung cancer, and felt instantly transported to a girder fifteen stories above street level with nothing to grab onto but wind. I needed to talk to someone. It hadn't yet occurred to me to speak to a spiritual advisor, and psychologists aren't covered by health insurance in Ontario. I went to see a psychiatrist. He seemed no more interested in the significance of my life experiences than Dr. X had been all those years before. Instead, he suggested that I try a drug called Effexor, because he had a whack of free samples in his desk drawer. He knew I had no benefits plan. Also, he added, "It has very few side effects."

"How does it work?" I remember asking.

"We don't know how it works," he answered, and that was true. The function of neurotransmitters in regulating emotion is only dimly understood. It remains entirely unclear, for one thing, why an antidepressant would act to calm anxiety, which is a radically different physiological experience than depression.

"If you don't know how these drugs work," I wondered to Dr. K., "then how do you know what they'll do to my brain chemistry in the long run?"

"Patricia," he replied, and his voice softened, grew gentle and mellifluous, "what do you think stress will do to your brain in the long run? You need to take medication. Your anxiety disorder isn't going to go away. You have to think of these drugs the way a diabetic thinks about insulin." Interestingly, I've heard that line since, several times. I wonder where Dr. K. got it, for it has the flavor of high-concept marketing. Did the drug rep who supplied him with free samples of Effexor provide him with the analogy? Back in 2002, though, it seemed to me that if Dr. K. thought I was the psychological version of a diabetic, I should resign myself to that fate—for the sake of my children, if nothing else. Dr. K. was very adamant on this point, that Clara and Geoffrey needed a brave, clearheaded, and high-functioning mother, and on this note he persuaded me to head for the pharmacy to fill out a prescription for a drug that I would wind up addicted to for five years.

Have you ever tried Ecstasy, or heroin? How about Xanax, or Placidyl, the sedative on which former U.S. Supreme Court chief justice William Rehnquist was reported to be heavily "reliant" for nine years? Any of the opiate or sedative drugs will lend you a sense of how my druggy relief was immeasurably sweet at the start. It felt heaven-sent. Waking up in the predawn hours, in the peaceful silence of my home, I felt a profound sense of safety. My children were sleeping soundly; the city was at rest. All were joined in an unassailable purpose: to lie vulnerably down and to snooze. I was a citizen of Whoville on Christmas Eve, with no inclination to suspect the coming mischief of the Grinch. I treasured this early morning serenity. It was some kind of gift, in those first weeks on an antidepressant.

Alas, the sleepy sense of glory was brief. As my grief faded, the intense treasuring of peace began to fade too. After a spell of three months or so, I realized that I had come to feel nothing much, one way or another. Everything was fine, the way a tidied house is fine. Splendid, we've cleaned up the mess. So . . . now what? How do we proceed to inhabit this showroom?

I began to live in an emotional half-light, a state of being that was secure and yet largely disengaged. It reminded me of my sojourn as a bureaucrat in the mid-1980s in my first job out of college, when I took a position at Ontario's Ministry of Labour, ghost-writing letters for the minister. "Dear Person Whose Leg Was Mangled in a Wood Chipper," I would type on a typical day, "thank you for your letter protesting that the Worker's Compensation Law is a 'total joke.' I have forwarded your concerns to the appropriate department and asked them to respond to you shortly."

I did not enjoy this ghostwriting job, mostly because I spent the day responding to genuine human calamity by (a) pretending that I was someone else, and (b) lying. Yet, it was effortless. Paperwork and coffee breaks and lunch, all at a placid pace. I watched the clock a lot, waiting for it to hit five. "Dear Widow Whose Husband Drowned in a Vat of Toner at the Wallpaper Factory, thank you for—" Oh, five o'clock, gotta go.

This kind of apathetic insincerity came to define my new existence on Effexor. Pay the bills, oversee the children's crises in a faintly exasperated manner, hug the husband, breeze around doing this and that. I'd watch movies without being stirred by them, listen to music without real interest. In truth, I began to feel faintly sociopathic.

"The self that emerges from a depression through the use of Prozac," notes Alice Bullard, using the word Prozac generically to refer to all of these drugs, "is a mystified self rather than a mystical self. The drug offers a small island in the abyss; a bit of land in the deep chasm into which one's soul is disappearing. Slowly this bit of land grows until the abyss is covered over—covered over or filled in? What happens to the abyss? Is it simply hidden behind a facade? Can this 'land' built with drugs be real? If so, what is the nature of its reality?"

Reading Bullard's words, I was reminded of the figure of the Samyad in the book I'd been reading to Clara, E. Nesbit's *Five Children and It*. When the children realize that the amazing sand fairy they've discovered on the beach will grant them a wish, they ask to be beautiful. And he grants it, without bothering to advise them that in becoming beautiful, they will become unrecognizable to themselves.

Those who post to Web sites about antidepressants invariably remark upon the "emotional flat-lining," as one user put it. They talk of feeling "numb," of losing desire, of nonchalantly telling their bosses to "go fuck themselves" and then being "duly relieved of employment." (Been there, done that.) They concede that their lack of libido has marred their marriages, or relationships. They yearn for their sorrow back, because with it comes the intermittent prospect of joy. The journalist Seth Stevenson, writing for *Slate* magazine, described coming off of Paxil: "A new phenomenon has taken hold. When I get teary-eyed watching a horrid chick-flick on a cross-country flight, I recognize it: feelings. On Paxil, I barely noticed they were gone. Now that they're back, even overcompensating, I never want to lose them again. Bitterness, anger, jealousy, sadness: they all make me happy."

Interesting that we need this emotional texture. Why do sociopaths crave thrill-seeking behaviors? Why do psychopaths reach for the extremes of power and rush through murder? Apparently, it isn't in our nature to rest content with nothing. We are compelled to feel *something*. In one of the most perceptive imaginings of hell I've ever encountered, the novelist Kelley Armstrong assigned a group of serial killers to a small, bucolic village surrounded by meadows and daisies, where nothing ever happened and no victims wandered through.

I went back to Dr. K. He played with his Palm Pilot while he listened to my concerns. He has never taken drugs in his life, so his ontological expertise is a bit hazy on this point. But he studied me for signs of distress. "You look better," he said approvingly.

"Do I? Well, maybe that's because I don't care about a goddamn thing anymore. I wonder if you know how that feels?"

He did not. What he knew is that I came to him harrowed and now, drugged, my face looked more relaxed. I was no longer pacing. I had been calmed. He seemed to feel that he'd done his job.

Technically, what Dr. K. had done via his prescription pad was to shock my system with such a high level of serotonin (by preventing its "reuptake") that my brain cells had

had to compensate by dropping levels of dopamine, the neurotransmitter involved in feeling pleasure. This effect, which the Harvard psychiatrist Joseph Glenmullen calls the "Prozac backlash," refers to the way that our brains adapt to the overstimulation of one neurotransmitter by pulling back on the release of other key chemicals. The result of the dopamine drop in response to the serotonin flood is flattened mood, apathy, and loss of sexual desire, among other things. That is not the only result of forcing high levels of serotonin to circulate. Only about 5 percent of serotonin actually *resides* in the brain. The remainder circulates in our bloodstream, regulating the gastrointestinal tract, the genitalia, the heart, and the nervous system. This is why antidepressant users can feel nausea, develop tremors and tics, gain weight, have acid reflux, and experience other ailments.

The idea that people need antidepressants because they have a "chemical imbalance" in their brains has evolved into a sort of urban legend. People are depressed or anxious—so one person advises another, be they physician or sister-in-law, for levels of expertise don't seem to enter into who spreads the word—because their brain chemistry is out of whack. Sufferers have a "serotonin deficiency" that can be corrected by selective serotonin reuptake inhibitors (SSRIs) or, in the case of Effexor, serotonin and norepinephrine reuptake inhibitors (SNRIs). The pharmaceutical companies have encouraged people to believe this poodle-in-the-microwave pseudoscience because it suits them and their shareholders tremendously well. The makers of Paxil, for instance, ran a TV ad a few years ago that stated, "With continued treatment, Paxil can help restore the balance of serotonin."

The trouble with this soothing explanation, as several researchers and an increasing number of journalists are now pointing out, is that serotonin deficiency is an insupportable claim. (Think curative waters at nineteenth-century spas, and then more than double the consumer damage. Calculate it "times pi.") According to researchers with the U.S. National Institute of Mental Health, the fact that SSRIs may help to relieve depression or anxiety—although placebos have been shown to work nearly as well—"cannot be used as primary evidence for seratonergic dysfunction." Put another way, as physicians Jeffrey Lacasse and Jonathan Leo have, "the fact that aspirin cures headaches does not prove that headaches are due to low levels of aspirin." They add flatly: "There is no such thing as a scientifically established correct 'balance' of serotonin."

In 2004, both the FDA and Health Canada released warnings related to new concerns about SSRI use, having to do with serotonin-stimulated behavior. By this, they meant specifically agitation, hostility, insomnia, acute anxiety, suicidal ideation, and—here is the one that made me a fool—"disinhibition and emotional lability." Both federal agencies cautioned that all such behaviors were potential "adverse effects" of antidepressant drugs. The warning is sublimely dry. The lived experience careers from the tragic to the deeply embarrassing.

In my case, the warned-of adverse effect was triggered by adding Zyban (also known as Wellbutrin) to my usual dose of Effexor in an effort to quit smoking. Whereupon, "disinhibition and emotional lability" ensued! I promptly made a pass at my daughter's friend's *mother* at a neighborhood Christmas party, shortly after flirting with every married man in the room.

I have no memory of doing this; nor do I have the slightest idea how I got home that night. I assume that I walked, although I may have diverted my path and visited a brothel, or stolen stuff from the 7-Eleven. Since I was in what is apparently called a "walking blackout," the options for what I actually did with my time are pretty much limitless. Maybe I shot a cat. Luckily, I have several eyewitness reports from the Christmas party. My friend Paula, for instance, confiding, "We were really, really worried about you."

"Why? Because I'd just asked Fran to go upstairs?"

"No. I'd never seen you like that before. You weren't acting drunk. You were perfectly poised. It was like you were . . . psychotic. You were acting normal, but your behavior was totally abnormal."

"You mean, because I asked Fran to go upstairs?"

"Partly that," Paula agreed, laughing. Naturally, this had become a major source of amusement among the moms, that I'd hit on Fran. Nobody seemed to think that I'd come out of the closet, including me, for I'd also thrown my arms around Fran's ex-husband. My behavior was all the more startling for being so indiscriminate: "I'll go upstairs with anyone, really, anyone at all." The family pet. A peanut butter sandwich. My own husband would have been a good prospect if he hadn't been at home, sound asleep.

The Zyban went into the garbage the next day. I dearly wanted to jettison the Effexor while I was at it, but I didn't dare. By now, I was very familiar with the heroin-withdrawal-style experience of missing a single dose. A family friend who had forgotten her pills at home when she traveled for a week-end had fallen down and had a seizure in a department store. I was cowed. Like street addicts, I began putting off the struggle to come clean.

Spend a few nights on the Internet discussion sites devoted to antidepressant use, and you realize in some amazement how stranded people are as they try to cope with these meds. The citizenry comes to these so-called tea and sympathy sites in droves, from all over the world, looking for help. They preface their remarks by saying "My GP never warned me," or "the doctor doesn't seem to know what I'm talking about." They then provide one another warmly with advice, all of it based on hellish and hard-won experience rather than medical knowledge. There are tips for withdrawing by cutting up your pills with an X-Acto knife into ever de-creasing amounts. Suggestions are made about vitamin B supplements and certain diets rich in fish oil. Some swear by acupuncture, others by hypnosis. We find ourselves returned to the era of folk medicine in villages, but are only there, remarkably, because of the medical establishment's willed silence about the drugs themselves.

How can so many thousands of people, very possibly millions, have been abandoned by so many of the practitioners of medical science and been made to fall back upon rumors and whispers about how to manage their meds? At first, I could only think that these particular doctors needed to be in control, to fix what they're interested in fixing; they suspect that they'll lose control if they allow their patients to make an informed choice. "I can repair your illness, but you need to know that you'll become emotionally bland, sexually absent, likely fat, probably at risk of getting diabetes, and every time you miss a dose, you'll feel like you've been shocked with a cattle prod. It's up to you." They don't want it to be up to you. They don't trust your judgment. They think you're *nuts*. Intriguingly, the three female psychiatrists I happen to know are all much more circumspect with their prescription pads in dealing with the minor mental illnesses. But if there is a gender difference, I haven't found any specific studies on the subject.

More insight can be gleaned from attending the American Psychiatric Association's annual meeting, which I did in May 2006. At the APA, you are at once overwhelmed by the sense that the ninety-five hundred psychiatrists milling past the drug company booths in the convention center to attend their drug-company-sponsored symposia about what's going on with the latest drugs have completely lost perspective on what it ought to mean to practice psychiatry. A large number of psychiatrists have become, for all intents and purposes, pharmacists. Under pressure from insurance companies to apply a quick fix, and caught up themselves in the satisfaction of seeing their patients' swift chemical rebounds, they seem to have sidelined talk therapy as the treatment of choice. They dole out drugs. Often, the patients demand such drugs, having been seduced by the dreamy-happy images of the pharmaceutical companies' direct-to-consumer ads. Psychiatrists have also been seduced, often by misleading studies, manipulative research grants, free samples. It is no longer clear who is driving the practice of medicine in this realm.

"I asked them what they felt like being human sandwich boards," Jerome Kassirer, author of *On the Take: How Medicine's Complicity with Big Business Can Endanger Your Health*, told an audience at the conference, describing a similar meeting he'd been to where "ninety-five out of a hundred doctors were wearing pharmaceutical company lanyards." According to Kassirer, the former editor-in-chief of the *New England Journal of Medicine* and a professor of psychiatry at Tufts, "about a third of the people at this conference are in financial conflict of interest." In other words, they are being paid to research or promote a psychiatric drug, which is doubtless why none of the symposia at the 2006 meeting were devoted to discussing side effects or withdrawal issues. "When someone is conflicted, and gives you a talk about a drug," Kassirer asked, "how do you interpret the data? How do you know what's actually in their heads?"

Attending the sessions, I watched doctor after doctor flash a perfunctory disclosure about their financial ties at the outset of their PowerPoint presentations. They would then, for the most part, proceed to say exactly what they had printed on their slides, which was like watching an English movie with English subtitles. Virtually all of the talk was about drug cocktails. One psychiatrist, for instance, spoke of tossing people onto an atypical antipsychotic in addition to Effexor, and described the results as if he were yakking about having tinkered with his car on a holiday weekend. His posture was laid-back, his smile relaxed. He figured the antipsychotic Seroquel was a good mix with Effexor. I might differ with that assessment. The side effects of Seroquel? "You'll sleep until next Tuesday," notes Jerod Poore, who runs the consumer information site crazymeds.org. You might also develop diabetes. Seroquel was formulated for patients with schizophrenia, for whom such drugs have a very clear and important payoff. But with the antidepressants losing market share as they begin to go off patent, the pharmaceutical companies are pushing antipsychotics as their (profitable) alternative for treating those of us who are just struggling with life's exigencies. I spoke to a Manhattan psychiatrist who had worked with cops and firemen suffering from trauma after 9/11. She had supplied them with free samples of Seroquel, because that was all she'd been provided at her clinic. It bothered her a great deal.

At another APA session, a child psychiatrist from Minneapolis talked about prescribing Prozac to seven-year-olds, and how the most common side effect, other than stomachaches, was "motor activation," which means getting blazingly hyper. She described a second-grade patient of hers with OCD, who did very well on a low dose of Prozac. But when she increased the dose, he began chasing his father with a knife and threatening to "kill everybody in the world." The psychiatrist called this a "pharmacological mania," noted that she sees it "a lot," and concluded not that seven-year-olds should be kept off Prozac the way we parents keep them away from espresso and booze, but that children in this condition should be given a supplementary mood stabilizer. I wanted to stand up during the Q&A and ask, "Look, are you off your head?" But I knew that would just sound like barking in church.

The historian Edward Shorter calls the creed of this badly corrupted church "scientism," which is not to be confused with good science. "Scientism," he argued, talking initially about Prozac, "lay behind converting a whole host of human difficulties into the depression scale, and making all treatable with a wonder drug. This conversion (from good science to scientism) was possible only because clinical psychiatry had enmeshed itself so massively in the corporate culture of the drug industry. The result was that a scientific discipline such as psychiatry nurtured a popular culture of pharmacological hedonism, as millions of people who otherwise did not have a psychiatric disorder craved the new compound because it lightened the burden of self-consciousness while making it possible for them to stay slim."

Well, I don't know about the slim part.

In the summer of 2005, I resolved to come off Effexor. There is nothing in established research that fixes a date for stopping treatment with antidepressants. No one appears to have bothered to study the time frame for the use of SSRIs. Two months? Five years? Forever? There has been no commercial incentive to find out. The profits are indefinite if people stay on the drugs, and since drug companies fund the lion's share of clinical trials, as well as the lion's share of ongoing "medical education" to the tune of $1.1 billion in 2004, questions like "how long to treat?" get subsumed by marketing catchphrases like "think of it the way a diabetic thinks of insulin."

Did I taper off? Well, I thought so. I thought I understood the protocol that was familar to Dr. K. and his colleagues. Stepwise down, down, down, to 37.5 milligrams, all very slowly, then free fall. A friend had done it. It didn't occur to me that I couldn't follow the same path. I kept myself at the minimal 37.5 milligrams for a great many days, often skipping. Proving to myself: I'm not a junkie. Look at me, I can go a day or two without the fix. No problem now, I'm good. I think I'm good. At least, I'm hoping.

Very few doctors approach the subject of antidepressant

withdrawal with anything like the vigilance they would use to help heroin addicts or alcoholics. The mere fact that these are legal rather than street drugs seems to blind health practitioners to the possibility that they could be pernicious and addictive. The fact that 78 percent of Effexor users have difficulties with withdrawal wasn't exactly brought to my attention by official sources. I know what meth does. I hear various accusations leveled against pot. I find myself wondering why we know of long-term usage impacts only with unsanctioned drugs. A century ago, there was a deep blurring of distinction between legal and illegal drugs in terms of their efficacy for treating minor mental illness. Alienists had no better idea of what they were doing in stuffing mental patients full of laxatives or plunging them into insulin-induced comas than did gentlemen of the East India Company who were self-medicating with grains of opium and tablets of chloral. Freud prescribed cocaine. People drank absinthe in bars and had their teeth removed for "moon madness" in the asylums. Everything was experimental. The notion that doctors possessed the safe, nonaddictive therapeutics while lay people deviantly messed themselves up with sinful substances surfaced fairly gradually. Valium, after all, was one of the most addictive drugs of the twentieth century.

By the time I found myself on Effexor, however, the demarcation between approved and disdained drugs was as rigidly clear as the seventeenth-century boundary between clergy-sanctioned religious practice and crazy, renegade talking to God *directly* shit, such as the Puritans engaged in. Official drugs, by definition, were righteous and good. Our media dutifully and frequently report on all manner of ills associated with illegal drug use. Ecstasy fries your brain! Hash gives you splinters! Whatever the negative consequence, the data is available in a heartbeat. But these are all related to drugs that render us temporarily irrational. That is their main danger and threat. Where are the commensurate headlines about legal drugs? Why didn't I know what awaited me when I tried to come off of Effexor?

"Unfortunately," writes Harvard's Glenmullen, "in the last decade deceptive practices have become routine in the researching, publishing and marketing of psychiatric drugs, making it extremely difficult for patients and practicing physicians to get accurate, balanced information." He cites, for example, a GlaxoSmithKline "business plan guide" from 1997 that advised its sales reps to assure GPs and psychiatrists that Paxil withdrawal "only occurs in 2 in 1,000 patients." The figure, Glenmullen says, is closer to six hundred.

The influence of the pharmaceutical companies is so profound that it has devolved upon a few activist psychiatrists like David Healy, Peter Breggin, and Joseph Glenmullen to simply provide users with a realistic plan to get off the drugs. Healy might have been my psychiatrist had circumstances been different. In 2000, the British-trained doctor had been offered a job at the University of Toronto, in association with the Centre for Addiction and Mental Health. Healy was to head up the mood and anxiety disorders program. But shortly before his move across the pond, he gave a speech on the University of Toronto campus that outlined his concerns about the heightened risk of suicide he and a few other experts were beginning to notice with antidepressant use. CAMH draws a considerable amount of its research funding from the pharmaceutical company Eli Lilly, makers of Prozac. Within two days of his speech, the University of Toronto told Healy that they were withdrawing their job offer; he was "not a good fit."

There is a little subindustry for psychiatrists to specialize in these days called plain old truth telling. In his self-help book *The Antidepressant Solution*, Glenmullen cites fifty-eight symptoms of withdrawal from the eleven major antidepressants, including anxiety, panic attacks, chest pain, and trembling. Drooling is another. For me, this involved suddenly having to spit out a large amount of saliva in the fitting room of a sporting goods store, with nothing at hand but Clara's just-bought can of Sprite.

Symptom 19: Confusion or cognitive difficulties, which involved warning my son, one evening, that if he didn't brush his teeth, right now, he was headed for another cavity and I'd have to call Mr. Hamster.

"Mr. who?" my husband asked, chuckling.

"I'm sorry, I mean Dr. Katchky."

After that, things grew less comical. My withdrawal featured night sweats, muscle aches, and shortness of breath. There were the electric pulses, but I was used to those from the times I'd missed a dose. (Seth Silverman in *Slate* best described them as feeling like someone had removed your skull cup and dragged a staticky blanket across your naked brain.) I became hugely, wildly irritable, so that what would usually be a one-day affair of PMS grrr-ing at everyone and everything carried on without respite. On most days, I felt a sort of hypercaffeinated whirring and buzzing sensation, a feeling of continuous adrenal rush. It was like being mildly electrified. And then, on certain days, it was as if someone had pulled the plug from the socket and the energy simply winked out. I experienced nothing but darkness, an unbearable density and weight that almost brought me to my knees. I had never felt this way in my life. Pushing my cart around the supermarket, listening to James Taylor's "Fire and Rain" played unobtrusively low, I concluded that if I heard him one more time, in one more snacks aisle, then both he and I were going to have to be shot.

On the Internet, I found similar astonished concerns: "I was a former meth user and I tell you," one woman wrote, "it was easier to get off that stuff." Posted another: "I am so angry with my dr's right now. I was on for 3 years and did a VERY slow taper off (3 months) and have been completely off for 4 days now. For the past 2 days I have been falling, dizzy, and violently vomiting. If I had known that this would happen when I tried to go off this horrible drug, I NEVER would have started."

"I have been Effexor free since April of this year and I'm doing great!" another woman posted reassuringly. "I did it on my own, after trying for 3 years with no success. I started to open the capsules each morning and I would take out one extra granule each day. It was a pain in the ass! However, it was the easiest method."

"People just *loathe* Effexor," says Jerod Poore, "because the discontinuation can be so harsh; it's the med everyone wishes they never took. People will change doctors because some doctor had the nerve to punish them with Effexor."

One night, four months into the withdrawal, I climbed into my husband's lap and burst into tears. I was exhausted by the effort of being sane. I did not know what to do. Clara—hearing me, or merely sensing something—woke up and peered into our bedroom. "Go back to bed, sweetie," Ambrose urged. And she did, but I have this vision of her remembering me in that pose as an iconic image of her childhood: the night she found her mother curled up and limp, in tears, like the little girl that she wasn't supposed to be in this house that needed, instead, a grown-up mother. Unwilling to expose Clara to my vulnerability any further, I asked Dr. K. to put me on something else. Not Effexor, but something that would enable me to recover from Effexor withdrawal until I could figure out what to do with the addiction. I went on a ten-milligram dose of the SSRI Lexapro and returned to the twilit world of No Emotion.

Over the past twenty or thirty years, as the use of antidepressants has soared in Western nations, the World Health Organization has sponsored a number of studies on treatment and recovery rates for mental illness around the globe. What has been found, consistently, is that patients in the developing world, in nations like India for example, are recovering better from their anguish and madness than people in the first world. One reason for this, argues medical anthropologist Murphy Halliburton, is that developing countries do not rely exclusively upon psychiatry for healing. While some of the early WHO-sponsored studies contained a typically Western disdain for "superstitious beliefs about mental illness," Halliburton says that "it may be precisely because people also go to 'faith healers,' or, more precisely, that patients have available a variety of therapeutic choices" that they reclaim their balance more quickly. Halliburton has done field research in the Indian state of Kerala, where people suffering from a range of afflictions, including schizophrenia and psychosis, are as likely to choose Ayurvedic medicine or religious healing (at mosques, temples, and churches) as they are to choose Western-style psychiatry. Each of these approaches has valence; none is subcultural or alternative to the others.

Is it possible, I find myself wondering upon reading Halliburton's research, that I could relinquish extreme anxiety through visits to the church down the street from my house? Maybe, or maybe not. Not precisely. The conservative wish is that the genie be stuffed back in the bottle, but that is not likely to happen. It contravenes the forces of social history. After every revolution, eventually, institutions and rituals and myths are woven together in a new and fitting way. You cannot go back, but you can circle back to collect what you've lost, what you've dropped. You can say, as the people in developing nations like India are invited to say: maybe there was wisdom here. Maybe this should continue with us on our journey.

9

Enough Screaming Like a Girl

Don't look for the remedy for your troubles outside yourself.
You are the medicine.
You are the cure for your own sorrow.

—RUMI, "THE JOURNEY STARTS HERE"

M Y SOUL IS ALARMED, said King David.
How do you quiet the soul?

With drugs? Through forgetfulness? By shopping, or winning fame? Plan super-prudently for the pandemic flu. Assign your fear to green peas. Or deny that you even have a
soul: banish it with reason, drown it with alcohol, lose it in
the ecstasies of orgasm. Pick a fight with your neighbor, or a
neighboring nation. Avowedly, determinedly assert control.

I've run through the options.

It is June 2007. I am sitting on a bench near a little waterfall,
beneath a slender maple sapling, gazing at a pretty English garden tangle of forsythia and honeysuckle. I've just been to the
library, on a part of the University of Toronto campus that I
never knew before, or never noticed, when I was a student

twenty years ago, a serene space between the theology school of Emmanuel College and the buildings of Catholic Saint Mike's. The shivering ivy covering the walls of Emmanuel is so thick that when the wind stirs, it creates a captivating optical illusion, in which the building appears to breathe.

My grandparents Maryon Moody and Lester Pearson met here, on this small, tranquil acre of the world. He was teaching history, and she was his lively student. She got his name wrong in her diary, the first time: called him Leslie. As a student here, himself, newly returned from World War I, he lived at the Delta Upsilon fraternity house up around the corner on Bloor Street. "On March 8, 1919, the fraternity's annual banquet was held at the Queen's Hotel," notes his biographer John English. "On the back of the evening's program was a brief homily from the theologian Henry Ward Beecher: "It is not work that kills men; it is worry. Work is healthy . . . Worry is the rust upon the blade."

Decades later, my grandfather returned to the campus as its chancellor after serving as president of the UN's General Assembly, and gave the June commencement speech to a cohort of young hopefuls fussing with their black-tasseled hats in the early summer breeze. "Freedom alone is not enough," he said in that speech, "if it is merely the right to live and work and have our being with a minimum of interference. It must include the obligation to be socially useful, and to take part in the struggle against evil and injustice. Only on that concept of freedom can a free and secure society be based." He spoke with a surprisingly high, light voice, my grandfather, not unlike Truman Capote's. He was diminutive like Capote as well. And charming and trenchant, with a backbone of steel. "Let us give the student a faith, a sense of mission, an understanding of social and moral values," he went on. "This will never be found in any single 'ism' of today, in socialism or profitism or materialism. It will never be found in developing or training a man's faculties merely for his own service."

Sitting on my bench in his shadow, I imagine myself starting at square one, graduating all over again, before the travesty of my twenties began. Maybe I could have lived better through my age of anxiety if I'd heard his speech; or maybe the point is that I need to start living better now: "with faith, a sense of mission, an understanding of social and moral values." The crucial freedom entailed in diminishing rather than aggrandizing my Self.

It has been six weeks since I came off of the antidepressant Lexapro. At first, as I tapered the dose, there was daily a kind of clean and piercing anguish, felt primarily when I woke up in the morning, a sensation that is known, in the scant literature on SSRI withdrawal, as "rebound anxiety." It's a surpassingly strange feeling because it is so purely physical. There are no racing thoughts involved, no panicked formulations. The mind remains calm even as the body gives off five-alarm signals of distress. You can engage the signals, or you can observe them as if from a distance, bemused. I practiced what Jon Kabat-Zinn calls mindfulness, feeling my breath flow in and out, observing every part of myself—my legs on the cotton sheets, my fingers lightly entwined in my hair, my cheek against the pillow, hearing beyond my window the musical chitter of robins. I reminded myself of what Kabat-Zinn says about self-efficacy: "Your confidence in your ability to grow influences your ability to grow."

After a while, I got used to the disquiet of my mornings and chose to think of the experience as living with back pain or some other chronic ailment. One night, the rebound anxiety staged a final hurrah, ridiculously enough while I was watching Eric Idle perform a comic oratorio based on *The Life of Brian*. There Idle was on stage, leading the Toronto Symphony Orchestra and the Mendelssohn Choir in a rousing rendition of Monty Python's iconic song, and all I could hear was the keening, mosquito-like whine of my dread of nonbeing. The audience around me was screaming with laughter and singing along to the chorus: "always look on the bright side of life, ta dum, de dum de dum de dum." I shook my head and smiled in dismay.

During these first weeks, I also had nightmares, which is apparently quite typical with SSRI withdrawal. In one, I was being chased by a silvery brown grizzly bear from which I narrowly escaped by waking up. In another, I found myself draped languidly across a cushioned bench, outside, exposed to the majestic beauty of the Grand Canyon, awed by the play of light and the sweep of cliffs. Then it dawned on me that the bench was in midair, attached at one end, where my feet were, to the cliff wall. If I moved even an inch in any direction, I would fall for miles. The choking panic that I felt was extraordinary. I felt a perfect—a *Platonic*—sense of terror.

I was about to plummet to a canyon floor. Yet, if I didn't move, if I didn't make some attempt to get off this bench and reach the solid, red-baked clay of the cliff surface two yards away, I would be consigned to being a tense, still form with a fast-beating heart paralyzed forever on a plank in midair. These were my choices.

When the kids woke me up that particular morning, or the dogs or a fire engine or whatever mundane stirring it was, I sat up and felt an incredible sense of relief. I hadn't had to choose! But then, as I went about the comforting business of making Clara and Geoffrey their toast and eggs, and talking Clara through the opera of brushing her hair, I settled into an understanding of my dream. It was totally obvious. I *had* to choose, and no amount of being awake and preoccupied with fourth-grade hairdos was going to alter that goading truth. I could remain trapped by anxiety, or "shut in," as Kierkegaard said, or I could move through the anxiety by inching and shimmying along the bench, every muscle taut, until my fingers scraped at dust and earth, and I pressed my face to the ground and felt its new solidity. As Kurt Goldstein wrote, "Courage, in its final analysis, is nothing but an affirmative answer to the shocks of existence, which must be borne for the actualization of one's own nature."

Say yes. Patricia: you've run through the options, say yes.

Many years ago, I had a shock to my existence that really ought to have taught me that I could deal with whatever was thrown at me. It happened at my godmother Margaret's house in Cuernavaca on a very quiet night. I was all alone:

Margaret had invited me to stay there while she was in Canada, and her housekeeper, the dreaded and censorious Lupe, was away for Samana Santa, the holy week of Easter. Freed temporarily from being glared at, I was happily crouched over an escritoire in Margaret's living room, wholly lost to the world as I studied my computer screen and contemplated what I was writing. Where I sat in this standard Mexican bungalow—in which each room is connected by an outside pathway and garden—was about one foot from the window, with the glass concealed by a curtain.

I was, as I recall, listening to MC 900 Ft. Jesus on the CD player when, all at once, I heard a fist slam into the window by my desk. A resounding bang, just at my ear. The same punctuation of silence that I'd always feared as a child. Here it was, a perfect sense of peace and then all at once a boom, an attacking fist, an aggressive thrust of sound and vibration at the window. Without further ado, I was on my feet and hurling back the curtain in a rushing rage.

"Who the hell are you?" I roared into the tropical darkness. "What do you want?"

No answer came, so I ran to the door and kicked it open. I charged outside, yelling into the shadowy garden, goading my potential attacker. As it turns out, there was nothing out there that night that was as frightening as me, and it's entirely possible, in retrospect, that what had hit the window was a disoriented grackle. A lost bird. I'll never know, and it doesn't matter. What stays with me is how I responded. Instead of screaming like a girl, like Janet Leigh in the shower scene in *Psycho*, or her daughter Jamie Lee Curtis all knock-kneed in the closet in *Halloween*, there was me, a real woman, confronting danger with a clarifying rage.

Note this down for later, I might have told myself at the time. Understand it as a weapon in your arsenal.

Every Wednesday, at five P.M., I pay a visit to Dave, my gracious and observant young psychologist who practices cognitive behavioral therapy. Dave is the one who has been making me look at my bank receipts and the other odd places in which I've invested my fear. He works with me on getting rid of "automatic thoughts," which are the negative and catastrophic conclusions that the anxiety-prone find themselves leaping to before they've even engaged their conscious mind. Just as Kabat-Zinn and his fellow mindfulness practitioners make one mindful of one's body, cognitive therapists make one mindful of one's thoughts. Both approaches help to brace me for whatever comes along day to day. So does my physical strength, which I build (grudgingly) through visits to the gym. My children bring me pet worms and potted bean plants and demented art, which I receive as totems of their grounding love. And then there is ritual, which I'm newly attuned to the importance of and still tentatively attempting to create.

There is a church down the street from my house. A pretty little church with a diminutive congregation, struggling to stay afloat in our culturally mixed downtown neighborhood. The priest wafts too much incense about and makes too many baffling references to the parable of Job and the fig tree. I come home and practice the language, annnouncing to Ambrose: "And lo, I checked the phone messages that you hath not checked since Friday. And behold, you hath a message from the marketing director at A&P Groceries that you musteth return, for they are on deadline, and you hath not completed your cheese label task." I relish the idiocy. And I'm fully prepared to get used to it, for I have been idiotic all my life, an *utter fool*. Believing that the man I loved and lived with would honor me. Expecting my employers to cherish my work. Hoping that highlighting violence would make it comprehensible rather than toxic. Fearing cows, and bills. How is any of that, any of our present secular experience in this time of profound social transition, less intrinsically foolish than praying ritually, as one does in the church or the temple or mosque, for the health of one's family and friends, for the community and the nation and the planet?

I offer a modern update on Pascal's Wager. In the late seventeenth century, the French scientist Blaise Pascal, lamenting that greater faith could be placed in reason "if reason were only reasonable," encouraged his colleagues and friends to make a bet. Wager, he said, that there is a God, for what have you got to lose if there *isn't*? My version is somewhat different. Dare to be irrational (because guess what? you already are) and wager that your life has a purpose, a meaning, an overarching story. And imagine within yourself a light or spark or Lord that will show you the way.

Acknowledgments

This book owes its first debt of gratitude to Marion Garner at Vintage Canada, who responded to my rambling thoughts in the spring of 2004 in a coffee shop—about my interest in the history of ambition—by suggesting that I write, instead, a history of fear. It was a simple, succinct suggestion that was absolutely brilliant.

My agents, Paula Balzer and Sarah Lazin, responded to the suggestion and helped me to persuade the superb Gillian Blake at Bloomsbury and the amazing Anne Collins at Random House Canada to pay a living wage while I wrestled my rough beast to the ground. No writer could be more blessed than I am to commit her thoughts and scribbles into the collective hands of Balzer, Lazin, Blake, and Collins. What a powerhouse of intelligent, funny, and totally *aware* women. Louise Dennys did a brilliant final pass through the manuscript, so the blessings abound.

At some point, the rough beast rallied, Cujo-style, from its beaten-down stance, and the Canada Council for the Arts stepped in to help me shape the book a final time before my mortgage went into default. I am extremely grateful for the council's support, and hope that I've repaid them in kind with the quality of my work.

My ability to articulate dread and to place it within the larger realm of historic human experience would not have been possible without the elegant thinkers whose books I devoured as I prepared my own. In particular, I bow my head to the wonderfully eclectic mind of the cultural geographer Yi-Fu Tuan, whose *Landscapes of Fear* I first read ten years ago and just hungrily inhaled. Of equal importance, the inimitable cultural historian Marina Warner, whose research and analysis in *No Go the Bogeyman* has been groundbreaking, as, indeed, all of her books have been. Then, one of the great intellectual synthesists and fashionable cravat wearers of all time, the psychologist Rollo May, whose work on the ideas of anxiety deserves to be brought back into the spotlight. These three intellects were keystones for me.

Thank you to my smart yet loving critics, who read my writing or refined my speculations at various stages along the way: Joel Baird, Gillian Kerr, Diana Bryden, Dr. Pier Bryden, Russell Monk, Michael Alexander, Fran Piccaluga, Allison Beatty-Simpson, Patricia Hluchy, Leah Cherniak, Dr. Kristina Jones, Dr. Patricia Cavanaugh, Robin, Barbara, John and Patricia Hannah, Tassie Cameron, Elaine Evans; my sisters, Hilary, Katharine, and Anne Pearson; my mother, Landon; and my husband, Ambrose. Your insights are gifts that I treasure. (While I didn't much discuss the book with my brother, Michael, busy as he was with a new job and a brand-new teensy son, I thank him too for all his love.)

My father, Geoffrey, furnished me with the poetry I used in this book, as well as the biographies of said poets. That, along with humor, has been his great wellspring of pleasure.

I am grateful to the support I've received from the staff at Bloomsbury and Random House, especially from my long-time publicist Frances Bedford, and also Benjamin Adams, Greg Villepique, Kylie Barker, and copy editor Eric Thomas. Additional thanks to Michael Ignatieff, Barbara Moon, and Paul Tough for their parts in shaping my memoir of crime reporting.

Above all, I need to honor my own little family. Clara, now ten, and Geoffrey, at seven, have been remarkable in their patience for my writing, and Ambrose has made that patience possible. He has been the loving parent that our children comfortably trust and turn to on any given day, even when the upstairs door is closed 'cause "Mommy is working." Ambrose has enabled me to create this book, without a single snipe or snarl or backhanded remark, and there cannot be a woman in history who doesn't recognize the blessing of that.

Notes

Chapter 1: Let's Roll

1 **"I awoke morning after morning with a horrible dread"**
William James, *The Varieties of Religious Experience: A Study in Human Nature* (New York: New American Library, 1958), 229.

2 **Nearly 20 percent of the adult inhabitants of the Land of the Brave** Approximately forty million American adults ages eighteen and older, or about 18.1 percent of people in this age group in a given year, have an anxiety disorder. See R. C. Kessler, W. T. Chiu, O. Demler, and E. E. Walters, "Prevalence, Severity, and Comorbidity of 12-month DSM-IV Disorders in the National Comorbidity Survey Replication," *Archives of General Psychiatry* 62, no. 6 (June 2005): 617–27.

4 **"wakeful anguish"** John Keats, "Ode on Melancholy," in *The Poetical Works of John Keats* (London: Oxford University Press, 1937), 247.

6 **"for absolute predictive control"** Maria Miceli and Cristiano Castelfranchi, "Anxiety as an Epistemic Emotion: An

177

Uncertainty Theory of Anxiety," *Anxiety, Stress, & Coping* 18, no. 4 (December 2005): 291–319.

7   **According to the epidemiologist Michael Osterholm** Betsy Querna, "Avian Flu: We're Screwed if It Hits Soon," *U.S. News and World Report*, June 16, 2005.

9   **"Fear sharpens the senses"** Kurt Goldstein, *The Organism: A Holistic Approach to Biology Derived from Pathological Data in Man* (New York: American Book Company, 1939), 293.

9   **Recent MRI research has demonstrated** Myrna Weissman et al., "Offspring at High Risk for Anxiety and Depression," in *Fear and Anxiety: The Benefits of Translational* Research, ed. Jack M. Gorman (Arlington: American Psychiatric Publishing, 2004), 65–83.

10 **Karen Horney once noted** Karen Horney, *Our Inner Conflicts: A Constructive Theory of Neurosis* (New York: W. W. Norton & Company, 1992).

12 **"Anxiety," he wrote, "is afraid, yet it maintains a sly intercourse with its object"** Søren Kierkegaard, *The Concept of Dread*, trans. Walter Lowrie (Princeton: Princeton University Press, 1944), 92.

12 **"what one desires is freedom, which is to say selfhood"** Ibid., 124.

13 **Kierkegaard called his own era "the cowardly age"** Ibid., 107.

13 **According to data from the World Mental Health Survey** "Prevalence, Severity, and Unmet Need for Treatment of Mental Disorders in the World Health Organization World Mental Health Surveys," *JAMA* 291, no. 21 (June 2004).

See also the many publications of the WHO World Mental Health Survey Consortium archived or cited at: http:// www.hcp.med.harvard.edu/wmh/publications.php.

14　**As the environmental thinker Dave Pollard has written** January 8, 2004, on his blog, "How to Save the World." Blogs.salon.com.

Chapter 2:　Childhood Waves of Trust and Fear

15　**"Sleep, you black-eyed pig"** Cited by Marina Warner, *No Go the Bogeyman: Scaring, Lulling, and Making Mock* (London: Chatto & Windus, 1998), 198.

16　**high reactive temperament** See, for example, Jerome Kagan, *The Growth of the Child: Reflections on Human Development* (New York: W. W. Norton & Co., 1978).

16　**Researchers in Europe** Anja Riitta Lahikainen et al., "Child-Parent Agreement in the Assessment of Young Children's Fears," *Journal of Cross-Cultural Psychology* 37, no. 1 (January 2006): 100–117.

17　**the startle reflex is potentiated by darkness** See a discussion in Weissman, "Offspring at High Risk."

17　**"When adults try to recall their earliest fears"** Yi-Fu Tuan, *Landscapes of Fear* (New York: Random House, 1979), 15.

23　**"Fear came upon me," Henry James Sr. wrote** Henry James, *Society the Redeemed Form of Man and the Earnest of God's Omnipotence in Human Nature: Affirmed in Letters to a Friend* (Boston: Houghton, Osgood & Co., 1879), 44.

23   The god Pan was aptly imagined by the Greeks Yiannis
     Papakostas et al., "A Historical Inquiry into the Appropri-
     ateness of the Term 'Panic Disorder,'" *History of Psychiatry*
     14, no. 2 (2003): 195–204.

23   Anxiety sensitivity is thought to be a significant harbin-
     ger See, for example, Steven Taylor, ed., *Anxiety Sensitivity:*
     Theory, Research and Treatment of the Fear of Anxiety (London:
     Lawrence Erlbaum Associates, 1999).

24   Both are more important indicators of adult proneness
     Daniel Pine, "Pathophysiology of Anxiety: A Developmen-
     tal Psychobiological Perspective," in *Fear and Anxiety*, 88.

24   "the alarming possibility of being able" Kierkegaard, *Con-*
     cept of Dread, 40.

24   An American slave lullaby Cited in Warner, *No Go the Bo-*
     geyman, 198.

25   Marina Warner explains the ambiguous and faintly
     menacing content of lullabies Ibid., 199.

25   "the fairy tale frankly describes" Tuan, *Landscapes of Fear*,
     20.

26   13 percent of American children suffer See Deborah
     A. Lott, "New Developments in Treating Anxiety Disor-
     ders," *Psychiatric Times* 18, no. 9 (September 2001).

28   "From this moment on" Count Villiers de L'Isle-Adam,
     Isis (Paris: Librarie Internationale, 1862), 85.

29   children of parents with an anxiety disorder are consid-
     erably more likely Abby Fyer, R. Yehuda, E. B. Foa, et al.,
     "Stress-Induced and Fear Circuitry Disorders: Planning the
     Research Agenda for DSM-V." Symposium at the annual
     meeting of the American Psychiatric Association, Toronto,

May 2006. See also John M. Hettema et al., "The Structure of Genetic and Environmental Risk Factors for Anxiety Disorders in Men and Women," *Archives of General Psychiatry* 62 (2005): 182–89.

Chapter 3:   Class Notes on a Nervous Breakdown

36   **"I was run over by the truth one day"** Adrian Mitchell, "To Whom It May Concern," from *Out Loud* (London: Jonathan Cape Ltd., 1964).

40   **"Without a certain degree of stability"** Miceli, "Anxiety as 'Epistemic' Emotion," 291–319.

40   **"cued off by a threat to some value"** Rollo May, *The Meaning of Anxiety* (New York: Ronald Press Company, 1950; New York: Pocket Books, 1977), 140. Citations are to the Pocket Books edition.

40   **the existentialist's concept of the dread of "non-being"** See, for example, Paul Tillich, *The Courage to Be* (London: Nisbet & Co., 1952).

41   **"may consist of the loss of psychological or spiritual meaning"** May, *Meaning of Anxiety*, 49.

41   **anxiety amid college students is extremely high right now** Anxiety Disorders Association of America, "Anxiety Disorders on Campus: The Growing Need for College Mental Health Services," released as part of ADAA's annual conference, St. Louis, March 2007.

41   **the average college student in the 1990s was more anxious** Jean Twenge, "The Age of Anxiety? Birth Cohort

Change in Anxiety and Neuroticism, 1952–1993," *Journal of Personality and Social Psychology* 79 (2000). Twenge expanded on her findings in the 2006 book *Generation Me: Why Today's Young Americans Are More Confident, Assertive, Entitled—and More Miserable Than Ever Before* (New York: Free Press, 2006).

42 **"problems in intimate relationships"** Pamela Braboy Jackson and Montenique Finney, "Negative Life Events and Psychological Distress Among Young Adults," *Social Psychology Quarterly* 65, no. 2 (June 2002).

42 **Consider the developmental psychologist Eric Erikson's theory** See his discussion in Erik H. Erikson, "The Eight Ages of Man," chap. 7 in *Childhood and Society* (New York: Norton, 1950).

43 **Quarterlife Crisis Web site** See www.quarterlifecrisis.com.

44 **"Turning and turning in the widening gyre"** W. B. Yeats, "The Second Coming," originally published in *Michael Robartes and the Dancer* (Dublin: Cuala Press, 1920).

47 **Kierkegaard described this as getting caught, or "shut in"** Kierkegaard, *Concept of Dread*, 129.

48 **"[Anxiety] is cosmic"** May, *Meaning of Anxiety*, 181.

49 **In Greek mythology** Yiannis Papakostas et al. "A Historical Inquiry into the Appropriateness of the Term 'Panic Disorder,'" *History of Psychiatry* 14, no. 2 (2003): 195–204.

49 **A retroactive analysis of David** Liubov Ben-Noun, "Mental Disorder That Afflicted King David the Great," *History of Psychiatry* 15, no. 4 (2004): 467–76.

50 **By the tenth century, Christendom had a patron saint** Papakostas, "Historical Inquiry Into," 199.

NOTES

50 **Until the German clinician Emil Kraepelin came up with the classifications we still use** See the discussion of Kraepelin's role in Edward Shorter, *History of Psychiatry: From the Era of the Asylum to the Age of Prozac* (Toronto: John Wiley & Sons, 1998).

53 **the neurologist George Beard called the condition "neurasthenia"** As relayed in Elaine Showalter, *The Female Malady: Women, Madness, and English Culture 1830–1980* (New York: Pantheon Books, 1985), 143.

54 **Charcot recast hysteria as an affliction** Shorter, *History of Psychiatry.*

55 **Recently, neuropsychiatrists have been able to confirm through brain imaging** Erika Kinetz, "Is Hysteria Real? Brain Images Say Yes," *New York Times*, September 26, 2006.

56 **Jane Welsh Carlyle** *Letters and Memorials of Jane Welsh Carlyle*, James Anthony Froude, ed. (London: Longmans, Green, and Co., 1883), 143.

57 **As Shorter notes, these "supposed indications were nothing short of a triumph of public relations"** Ibid., 124.

58 **"The mind-cure principles are beginning so to pervade the air"** James, *Religious Experience*, 77.

59 **"Like her remembrance of awakened birds"** Wallace Stevens, "Sunday Morning," in *The Palm at the End of the Mind: Selected Poems and a Play*, Holly Stevens, ed. (New York: Vintage, 1990). Wallace Stevens was, or so critics contend, struggling in this poem with his Christian disenchantment and wanting to articulate his sense that the idea of God, or the formal construction of God, was no longer

workable, while the alternative vision remained ambiguous and unsettled, initially as manifestly satisfying as oranges and bright green playful birds on Sunday morning, and then something darker, pigeons circling down into darkness.

Chapter 4: A Life of Crime

61 **"We are like a lot of wild spiders"** Robert Lowell, "Fall 1961," from *For the Union Dead* (New York: Farrar, Straus & Giroux, 1964).

62 **"His courage bowls you over. His brutality makes you shudder"** Denis Diderot, *Rameau's Nephew* (New York: Penguin Classics, 1976), 93.

62 **and slowly our fear of criminality began to creep upward** " 'Lock 'Em Up!': Poll Indicates Fear of Crime Is Top U.S. Concern," *Current Events*, February 14, 1994.

63 **Between 1993 and 1994, during which time the serial killer Jeffrey Dahmer** Dennis T. Lowry, Tarn Ching Josephine Nio, and Dennis W. Leitner, "Setting the Public Fear Agenda: A Longtitudinal Analysis of Network TV Crime Reporting, Public Perceptions of Crime, and FBI Crime Statistics," *Journal of Communications* 53, no. 1 (March 2003): 61–73.

71 **Of psychologically healthy Vietnam vets** Judith Herman, *Trauma and Recovery: The Aftermath of Violence: From Domestic Abuse to Political Terror* (New York: Basic Books, 1992).

77 **"To cease wishing is to be dead . . ."** Rollo May, *Love and Will* (New York: W. W. Norton, 1974), 213.

Chapter 5: Fear's Geography

79 **"In a sense, every human construction"** Tuan, *Landscapes of Fear*, 87.

80 **Mexico has a much lower rate of clinically significant anxiety** WHO World Mental Health Survey Consortium, "Prevalence, Severity, and Unmet Need for Treatment of Mental Disorders," *JAMA* 291, no. 21 (June 2004).

80 **a person is four times more likely to suffer from generalized anxiety disorder in the United States than in Mexico** Ibid.

80 **Moreover, the *intensity* of anxiety gets more severe as you head north** Ibid.

80 **When Mexicans are beset by what they (and other Latin Americans) call *ataques de nervios*** For a discussion of the nature and quality of this folk illness, see Roberta D. Baer, Susan C. Weller, Javier Garcia de Alba Garcia, et al., "A Cross-Cultural Approach to the Study of the Folk Illness *Nervios*," *Culture, Medicine and Psychiatry* 27, no. 3 (2003): 315–37.

81 **when Mexicans migrate to Texas** See, for example, J. Breslau, S. Aguilar-Gaxiola, G. Borges, et al., "Mental Disorders Among English-Speaking Mexican Immigrants to the US Compared to a National Sample of Mexicans," *Psychiatry Research* 151, no. 1–2: 115–22. See also "U.S.-Born Mexican Americans and Non-Hispanic Whites at Increased Risk for Psychiatric Disorders: Findings Raise New Questions About Influence of Culture," *NIH News*, Dec. 6, 2004.

83   Rollo May once wrote, "Competitive individualism militates against the experience of community" May, *Love and Will*, 177.

83   the Mbuti Pygmies of the central African rain forest Tuan, *Landscapes of Fear*, 37. For a fuller description of the Mbuti, see also Colin M. Turnbull, *The Forest People* (New York: Simon & Schuster, 1961). A similar lack of fear has been noted in the Tasaday of the Mindanao rain forest in the Philippines, the Semang of the Malay Peninsula, and the !Kung Bushmen of the Kalahari Desert. (For whom "neurological diseases are rare, suicide is unheard of, and there is no stealing.") See Richard Lee and Irven DeVore, eds., *Kalahari Hunter-Gatherers: Studies of the !Kung San and Their Neighbors* (Boston: Harvard University Press, 1976), 171.

84   The historian Paul Newman speculates in *A History of Terror* Paul Newman, *A History of Terror: Fear and Dread Through the Ages* (London: Sutton Publishing, 2000), 65.

84   "Acute awareness of time is a cause of tension and distress in contemporary Western society" Tuan, *Landscapes of Fear*, 39.

87   But I have seen similar data suggesting that Nigerians See, for example, Michael Bond, "The Pursuit of Happiness," *New Scientist*, October 4, 2003. This article draws on the research of the World Values Survey, an ongoing collaboration between social scientists. The World Mental Health Survey Initiative has found a twelve-month prevalence rate for anxiety in Nigeria of 3.3 percent, about half that of Mexico, and one-sixth of the American prevalence rate. See *JAMA* 291, no. 21 (June 2004).

87 **Perhaps some light might be shed on this by Dr. Samuel Thielman** Samuel B. Thielman, "Religious and Spiritual Aspects of the Diagnosis of Anxiety Disorders and Adjustment Disorders," a symposium at the annual meeting of the American Psychiatric Association, Toronto, May 2006.

88 **"I'll never know why I got cancer"** Alice Lesch Kelly, "The Struggle to Move Beyond 'Why Me?'" *New York Times*, May 8, 2007.

88 **"It is not allowed that we live our lives in resignation to 'fate'"** Alice Bullard, "From Vastation to Prozac Nation," *Journal of Transcultural Psychiatry* 39, no. 3 (2002), 277.

89 **"Ritual," notes Tuan, "has this in common with scientific procedure"** Tuan, *Landscapes of Fear*, 176.

90 **Consider, for instance, the court records for "The People Versus Locusts"** E. P. Evans, *The Criminal Prosecution and Capital Punishment of Animals: The Lost History of Europe's Animal Trials* (Boston: Faber & Faber, 1906).

91 **Others were not so lucky: in 1394, a pig was hanged** Ibid., 156

91 **While I agree with Evans that these trials reflected the "hair-splitting and syllogistic rubbish"** Ibid., 89.

92 **"We have forgotten what it is like to be really and truly afraid of malevolent, disembodied spirits"** Timothy Taylor, *Buried Souls: How Humans Invented Death* (Boston: Beacon Press, 2005), 28.

93 **"Despite the inability of the world to end punctually"** Newman, *History of Terror*, 99.

94 **"Western parents indulge children's emotions and encourage them to pay a great deal of attention"** Carl

Ratner, "A Cultural/Psychological Analysis of Emotions" *Culture & Psychology* 6, no. 1 (2000): 5–39.

94 **The psychologist Ruth Chao has noted similar distinctions** Ruth Chao, "Chinese and European-American Cultural Models of the Self Reflected in Mothers' Child-Rearing Beliefs," *Ethos* 23, no. 3 (1995): 328–54.

95 **It is likely no coincidence that the Chinese also rank very low** World Mental Health Survey.

96 **"in the whirlwind of the Fiesta, we let go"** Octavio Paz, *The Labyrinth of Solitude and Other Writings* (New York: Grove Press, 2000) 153.

Chapter 6: When Murderers Scream at Spiders

97 **"And holy to his dread is that dark"** W. H. Auden, *The Age of Anxiety: A Baroque Eclogue* (New York: Random House, 1947), 95.

98 **a story that the BBC aired** "Why Do People Get Phobias?" March 24, 2006. See also "I'm Pea-Trified: Bizarre Frozen Veg Phobia Makes Mum's Life a Misery," *London Daily Mirror*, March 22, 2006.

99 **the phenomenon of koro** For a discussion, see Sonia Sarró and Vanessa Sarró, "Koro Syndrome: A Case Report," in *Transcultural Psychiatry* 41, no. 4 (December 2004): 558–60.

99 **In south India, people have been known to develop the terror that they're pregnant with a litter of puppies** A. N. Chowdhury et al., "Puppy Pregnancy in Humans: A Culture-Bound Disorder in Rural West Bengal, India,"

International Journal of Social Psychiatry 49, no. 1 (2003): 35–42.

101 **About 6 percent of North Americans have an "incapacitating" fear of animals** Martin Antony, *Overcoming Animal and Insect Phobias* (Oakland: New Harbinger Publications, 2005), 16.

101 **Shark phobias rose sharply after *Jaws* came out** Ibid., 27.

102 **"These findings," Beck says, "indicate that a person"** Aaron Beck and Gary Emery, *Anxiety Disorders and Phobias: A Cognitive Perspective*, rev. ed. (New York: Basic Books, 2005), 119.

104 **the case of a man who "feared going through swinging doors, driving his car, and disclosing business secrets"** Ibid., 123.

105 **"The disgusting can possess us"** William Ian Miller, *The Anatomy of Disgust* (Boston: Harvard University Press, 1997), 27.

106 **"when people were asked what disease they feared, only 5 percent named cancer"** Joanna Bourke, *Fear: A Cultural History* (London: Virago, 2006), 298.

106 **In general, women have more phobias than men** Antony and McCabe, *Animal and Insect Phobias*, 17.

109 **A 1984 study of blood phobics** Lars-Göran Öst, Ulf Sterner, Inga-Lena Lindahl, "Physiological Responses in Blood Phobics," *Behavior Research and Therapy* 22 (1984): 109–17.

111 **"cognitive distortions, visual imagery, and somatic imagery combine to magnify the actual danger"** Beck, *Anxiety Disorders and Phobias*, 128.

112 **This man, Jung said, "forced everything under the inexorable law of reason"** Carl Jung, *Psychology and Religion* (New Haven: Yale University Press, 1938), 18.

113 **the more a culture insists upon rational control** See, for example, several observations about this in Steven Friedman, ed., *Cultural Issues in the Treatment of Anxiety* (New York: Guilford Press, 1997).

113 **The American composer Allen Shawn** Allen Shawn, *Wish I Could Be There: Notes from a Phobic Life* (New York: Viking, 2007), 126.

115 **they also suffer to a significant degree from a culture-bound form of hysteria known as sleep paralysis** Cheryl Paradis and Steven Friedman, "Sleep Paralysis in African Americans with Panic Disorder," *Transcultural Psychiatry* 42, no. 1 (March 2005): 123–34. Specifically: "In a study of Nigerian civil servants and undergraduates, 58 percent revealed that they had one or more ISP events in the preceding year; 35.5 percent of subjects admitted experiencing ISP events at least twice during the preceding year. They understood this as being oppressed by evil spirits, and associated it with stress," 127.

115 **"hit by the wind"** James Boehnlein, "Cultural Interpretations of Physiological Processes in Post-Tramautic Stress Disorder and Panic Disorder," *Transcultural Psychiatry* 38, no. 4 (December 2001): 461–67. See also Devon Hinton et al., "Hit by the Wind and Temperature-Shift Panic Among Vietnamese Refugees," *Transcultural Psychiatry* 40, no. 3 (September 2003): 342–76.

116 **The anthropologist Robert Lemelson** Robert Lemelson, "Obsessive Compulsive Disorder in Bali: The Cultural Shaping of a Neuropsychiatric Disorder," *Transcultural Psychiatry* 40, no. 3 (September 2003): 377–408.

117 **one study of Egyptian adolescents** Ahmed Okasha, "OCD in Egyptian Adolescents: The Effect of Culture and Religion," *Psychiatric Times* 21, no. 5 (April 2004).

119 **Recalled William James of his period of extreme anxiety** James, *Varieties of Religious Experience*, 136.

Chapter 7: Fear of Failure, Fear of Success: Anxiety in the Workplace

120 **"[Fame] boils down to immortality"** Damien Hirst and Gordon Burn, *On the Way to Work* (New York: Universe Publishing, 2002), 51.

122 **According to a 2006 survey** See www.adaa.org, "Americans Report Stress and Anxiety On-the-Job Affects Work Performance, Home Life," News release, November 8, 2006.

123 **Between 2001 and 2004, approximately 3.5 million Americans** Lisa Mainiero and Sherry Sullivan, *The Opt-Out Revolt: Why People Are Leaving Companies to Create Kaleidoscope Careers* (Mountain View, CA: Davies-Black Publishing, 2006), 82.

123 **Sullivan and Mainiero quote the management consultant Peter Drucker** Ibid., 18.

124   **"women are persistently excluded from the social decision-making networks"** Ibid., 45.

124   **In last year's advice book** *Am-BITCH-ous* Debra Condren, *Am-BITCH-ous* (New York: Morgan Road Books, 2006).

125   **workers who exhibit "neuroticism"** Thomas Ng, Lillian Eby, Kelly Sorensen, and Daniel Feldman, "Predictors of Objective and Subjective Career Success: A Meta-Analysis," *Personnel Psychology* 58 (2005): 367–408. See also Melissa Osborne Groves, "How Important Is Your Personality? Labor Market Returns to Personality for Women in the US and UK," *Journal of Economic Psychology* 26, no. 6 (2005): 827–41.

125   **a 2005 study "Can Worriers Be Winners?" concluded** Adam M. Perkins and Philip J. Corr, "Can Worriers Be Winners? The Association Between Worrying and Job Performance," *Personality and Individual Differences* 38, no. 1 (2005): 25–31.

125   **Seventy-nine percent of workers responding to a poll** Ipsos Reid for the Global Business and Economic Roundtable on Addiction and Mental Health. Data released at a news conference in Washington, February 15, 2007.

126   **now speak in terms of "psychological capital"** See, for example, Frederick P. Morgeson, Matthew Reider, and Michael Campion, "Selecting Individuals in Team Settings: The Importance of Social Skills, Personality Characteristics, and Teamwork Knowledge," *Personnel Psychology* 58, no. 3 (2005): 583–611.

127   **Mental and emotional problems at work** Study commissioned by the Canadian Business and Economic Roundtable on Mental Health and released to media on October 4, 1999.

127 **"the super-competent and self-possessed person of the modern world"** Alice Bullard, "Vastation to Prozac Nation," 277.

128 **employees are also less likely to be promoted** Thomas Ng et al., "Predictors of Objective and Subjective."

128 **"Staring at other people, for example, especially one's elders"** Donald Capps, *Social Phobia: Alleviating Anxiety in an Age of Self-Promotion* (St. Louis: Chalice Press, 1999), 193. See also Sumie Okazaki, "Expressions of Social Anxiety in Asian-Americans," *Psychiatric Times* 20, no. 10 (October 2003).

132 **"Around here you've got to be smart, and people know how to manipulate"** Gary Strauss, "How 'Opal Mehta' got shelved," *USA Today*, May 7, 2006.

133 **The poet Paul Muldoon relates a very funny story** Paul Muldoon in Robin Robertson, ed., *Mortification: Writers' Stories of Their Public Shame* (New York: Harper Perennial, 2005).

134 **Surveying the research on creative intelligence and emotional health** Dean Keith Simonton, "Are Genius and Madness Related? Contemporary Answers to an Ancient Question," *Psychiatric Times* 22, no. 7 (June 2005).

134 **William Butler Yeats was a visionary** Richard Ellmann, *Yeats: The Man and the Mask* (New York: W. W. Norton & Co., 1999), 78.

135 **"The best lack all convictions"** From Yeats's poem "The Second Coming."

135 **Creatively gifted individuals in general** Simonton, "Are Genius and Madness Related?" See also: H. S. Akiskal, "In

Search of Aristotle: Temperament, Human Nature, Melancholia, Creativity and Eminence," *Journal of Affective Disorders*, May 2007.

135 **"creativity requires the cognitive ability and the dispositional willingness"** Simonton, "Are Genius and Madness Related?"

136 **Among history's most inspired and lasting creators** As noted by Kay Redfield Jamison, *Touched with Fire: Manic-Depressive Illness and the Artistic Temperament* (New York: Free Press, 1996).

137 **In their 2006 book, *The Power of Nice*** Linda Kaplan Thaler and Robin Koval, *The Power of Nice: Eight Ways to Kill the Business World with Kindness* (New York: Doubleday, 2006).

137 **"you often hear about the term 'fake it 'til you make it'"** Ibid., 62.

137 **a survey of fifteen thousand American managers** Sullivan and Maniero, *Opt-Out Revolt*, 184.

138 **"I learned very early"** R. Buckminster Fuller, *Critical Path* (New York: St. Martin's, 1982), 225.

Chapter 8: 2001: A Drugs Odyssey

139 **"Bright, energetic, not too serious, not too thoughtful"** Bullard, "Vastation to Prozac Nation," 281.

139 **"The antidepressant Catch-22"** Joseph Glenmullen, *The Antidepressant Solution: A Step-by-Step Guide to Safely Overcoming Antidepressant Withdrawal, Dependence, and "Addiction"* (New York: Free Press, 2005), 15.

145 **Placidyl, the sedative on which former U.S. Supreme Court chief justice William Rehnquist** For a full report on Rehnquist's addiction, see Jack Shafer, "Rehnquist's Drug Habit: The Man in Full," *Slate*, January 5, 2007.

147 **"The self that emerges from a depression through the use of Prozac"** Bullard, "Vastation to Prozac Nation," 282.

147 **The journalist Seth Stevenson, writing for *Slate* magazine** Seth Stevenson, "Extroverted Like Me: How a Month and a Half on Paxil Taught Me to Love Being Shy," *Slate*, January 2, 2001.

148 **In one of the most perceptive imaginings of hell** Kelley Armstrong, *Haunted* (New York: Bantam, 2005).

149 **This effect, which the Harvard psychiatrist Joseph Glenmullen** Ibid.

149 **Only about 5 percent of serotonin actually *resides* in the brain** Ibid.

150 **The makers of Paxil, for instance, ran a TV ad** See discussion of this and other pharmaceutical ads in Jeffrey Lacasse and Jonathan Leo, "Serotonin and Depression: A Disconnect between the Advertisements and the Scientific Literature," *PLoS Med* 2, no. 12 (Nov. 8, 2005).

150 **According to researchers with the U.S. National Institute of Mental Health** Ibid.

150 **placebos have been shown to work nearly as well** Irving Kirsch and David Antonuccio, "Antidepressants Versus Placebos: Meaningful Advantages Are Lacking," *Psychiatric Times* 19, no. 9 (September 2002).

150 **Put another way, as physicians Jeffrey Lacasse and Jonathan Leo have** Ibid.

156 **The historian Edward Shorter calls the creed** Shorter, *History of Psychiatry*, 324.

157 **the lion's share of ongoing "medical education"** Daniel Carlat, founding editor of *The Carlat Report*, in an address about conflicts of interest in medical education at the annual meeting of the American Psychiatric Association, Toronto, May 2006.

159 **"Unfortunately," writes Harvard's Glenmullen** Joseph Glenmullen, *Antidepressant Solution*, 199.

159 **A few activist psychiatrists like David Healy** See, for example, David Healy, *Let Them Eat Prozac* (London: James Lorrimore & Co., 2003); Glenmullen, *Antidepressant Solution*; Peter Breggin and David Cohen, *Your Drug May Be Your Problem: How and Why to Stop Taking Psychiatric Medications* (Reading: Perseus Books, 1999).

160 **the University of Toronto told Healy** Healy, *Let Them Eat Prozac*, 312.

160 **Glenmullen cites fifty-eight symptoms** Glenmullen, *Antidepressant Solution*, 84.

162 **"People just *loathe* Effexor," says Jerod Poore** See Poore and colleagues' detailed descriptions of the pros and cons of a wide range of psychiatric meds, including Effexor, at www.crazymeds.org.

162 **the World Health Organization has sponsored** See, for example, T. J. Craig, C. Siegel, K. Hopper, S. Lin, and N. Sartorius, "Outcome in Schizophrenia and Related Disorders Compared Between Developing and Developed Countries. A Recursive Partitioning Re-analysis of the WHO DOSMD Data," *British Journal of Psychiatry* 170 (1997): 229–33.

K. Hopper and J. Wanderling, "Revisiting the Developed Versus Developing Country Distinction in Course and Outcome in Schizophrenia: Results from ISoS, the WHO Collaborative Followup Project," *Schizophrenia Bulletin* 26, no. 4 (2000): 835–46.

For a rejoinder, specifically about a major mental illness like schizophrenia, see Vikram Patel, Alex Cohen, Rangaswamy Thara, and Oye Gureje, "Is the Outcome of Schizophrenia Really Better in Developing Countries?" *Revista Brasileira de Psiquiatria* 28, no. 2 (June 2006).

163 **One reason for this, argues medical anthropologist Murphy Halliburton** Murphy Halliburton, "Finding a Fit: Psychiatric Pluralism in South India and Its Implications for WHO Studies of Mental Disorder," *Transcultural Psychiatry* 41, no. 1 (2004): 80–98.

Chapter 9: Enough Screaming Like a Girl

165 **"Don't look for the remedy"** Rumi, "The Journey Starts Here," Nevit O. Egin, trans., in *The Forbidden Rumi: The Suppressed Poems of Rumi on Love, Heresy and Intoxication* (Inner Traditions Press, 2006).

166 **On March 8, 1919** John English, *Shadow of Heaven: The Life of Lester Pearson* (Toronto: Lester & Orpen Dennys, 1989), vol. 1, p. 59.

166 **"Freedom alone is not enough"** Family papers.

168 **what Kabat-Zinn says about self-efficacy** Jon Kabat-Zinn, *Full Catastrophe Living: Using the Wisdom of Your Body*

and Mind to Face Stress, Pain, and Illness (repr. New York: Bantam Dell, 2005), 201.

169 **"Courage, in its final analysis"** Kurt Goldstein, *The Organism: A Holistic Approach to Biology* (New York: American Book Company, 1939), 306.

172 **"if reason were only reasonable"** Blaise Pascal, *Pensées*, trans. W. F. Trotter (New York: Courier Dover Publications, 2003), 22.

A Note on the Author

PATRICIA PEARSON is the author of four previous books, including the groundbreaking *When She Was Bad*, a study of female aggression that won the Arthur Ellis award for best nonfiction crime book of 1997. Her novel *Playing House* was shortlisted for the Stephen Leacock Memorial Medal for Humour and was adapted for television. A member of *USA Today*'s board of op-ed writers, she has written commentary for a number of publications, including the *New York Times*, the *Guardian*, the *Times* (UK), as a weekly columnist for Canada's *National Post*, and through her blog, *Good News About the Coming Apocalypse*. She speaks frequently on media issues and on the role of humor in allaying anxiety and stress. She lives in Toronto.